YOUR SUBCONSCIOUS POWER

How to Make It Work for You

CHARLES M. SIMMONS

YOUR

SUBCONSCIOUS

POWER

How to make it
work for
~~~~~~~~~~~~~~~~~~~~~~~YOU~~~~~~~~

Melvin Powers
Wilshire Book Company

12015 Sherman Road, No. Hollywood, CA 91605

ISBN 0-87980-178-6

Dedicated to our son
CHARLES M. SIMMONS, II
who has been a constant inspiration
and challenge to me

Table of Contents

PART 1 | YOUR PLAN

1 What is Life?   3

*Is life a question mark?—This is your life—Let
your subconscious have control—Choose a new
life—Your subconscious is a source of power—
Life is influenced action*

**2 You are the Most Important Person
in the World**   10

*"I . . . My . . . Me!"—Humbleness is unbecoming—The creator made you different—Being important is your right—Satisfy your inner urges—
No one is more important than you—Your name
packs power—Be influenced the positive way—
—Subconscious power in action!*

**3 The Dynamic Factor which Master-Controls
Your Life**   19

*Applaud yourself—Part of your life is in this book
—What is really controlling your life—Don't be a
living puppet—You can achieve positive results—
Depend on yourself first—Everything you do is
important—Science has paved the way—The best*

people are self-influenced—Leaders are self-influenced—Interesting people are self-influenced—Success comes from self-influence—Self-influence for yourself

4   Self-Influence is the Key to
    the Pattern of Your Life   31
    Don't be a fenced-in slave—Your three steps of learning—The beginning of a good experience—The choice is yours—Stimulating and inspiring prospects—Make a pact with yourself—Remember your agreements

5   Is Life a Mystery?   40
    To him who has shall be given—People make life a mystery—Focus your faith on your whole life—Self-influence builds up faith—To understand yourself, understand others—There are people with wrong motives—Faith in others brings faith in life—Distinctiveness is your birthright—Does God help those who help themselves?—Join the club

6   Is there a Superior Race in the Making?   50
    The person you see in the mirror—Making men masters of themselves—The power that is building up—Progressiveness is in the air—Many people need help—Participation pays off—An invitation to progress—Service to others is good business—Become a member

PART 2 | YOUR PRACTICE

7   The Latest Models in Human Beings   61
    What model are you?—Being objective pays divi-

dends—Choose your model—Many people are like this model—Here's a model you see often—This one matches people you know—This model looks better than it acts—You see this model stalled quite often—Here's the most wanted model—You can be the model you choose—Trade in that old model

8 **The Subconscious Mind is the Key to Self-Influence** 69

A million dollar value—Stop! Look! Listen!—Visit your private world—You know yourself better—Face this question boldly—The effects of wrong influence—Good things aren't cheap—A perfect partnership—Don't go it alone—You can be a creator and a controller—Subconscious self-influence is the key

9 **A Trip into "Inner Space"** 79

Outer space is coming closer—Wonderful new horizons ahead—A fascinating inner world—Let's go into inner space—A bright, lively place—What controls this inner world—Your conscious mind in action—The center of power in your mind—Be aware of this power—Values are measured subconsciously—Habits are subconsciously controlled—Noteworthy action from noteworthy thoughts—Every experience labeled "positive" or "negative"—Your remarkable will—Turn on the power

10 **The Subconscious Mind: "A Garden of Eden" or a "Purgatory"** 91

Escape from humdrum living—Your habits on display—Why you put things off—Watch out for negative influences—Lack of control brings fear—Bystanders get no dividends from life—Habits acquired in two ways—Your life at the balance point—Your Garden of Eden

11   The New Positive Concept of Self-Control   100
      *Sign your life away!—A new creed of living—Don't
      be normal—Be above normal—Put a plus sign on
      yourself—This is the turning point—Follow
      through on your creed—New attitudes—New
      habits—Tonight is the night!—Tomorrow will be
      bright—Stop here and enjoy life*

12   Science and the Subconscious Mind   109
      *Get the answers! Know the facts!—The role of sci-
      ence in society—Lay people apply science—Sci-
      ence is part of your life—Lay people cause scien-
      tific progress—More lay scientists needed—Apply
      scientific principles yourself—Research is the basis
      for this knowledge—Professional use of subcon-
      scious influence—Modern knowledge is the basis
      of this book—We are partners with scientists—
      Answer your questions—Part of you never sleeps—
      24-hour use of subconscious power—You are a
      psychologist*

13   How to Use the Power of Your Subconscious   121
      *A new kind of personal power—You have used this
      power at times—This power was demonstrated
      just yesterday—Only one source of inner power—
      Inner power from knowledge—Strength from
      inner power—How to turn on inner power—Go on
      a retreat to start right—Avoid trial and error ideas
      —Be positive! Be deliberate!—Use your tireless
      subconscious*

14   The Subconscious Mind and Your Past   130
      *Your past has great value—Is life a privelege, or a
      responsibility?—Consider your whole life—Your
      past is a rich resource—Just what has happened
      in the past?—A self-portrait of you—The "zeros"
      in your past are important—Why your past is re-*

corded as it is—What you have been responsible for—Now you know the whys and wherefores—Any change is your responsibility

15 **The Subconscious Mind and Your Present** 139
Face the present squarely—That will of yours—Your past and your present—You can define the effects—The determining balance

16 **The Subconscious Mind and Your Future** 144
You can see the future clearly—You will control your future—The future will be different—The pattern of your future is in your hands—Not the same old way of life—New paths lead into the future—Objectives are important—Your dreams can come true

PART 3 | PERFECTION

17 **You and Your Subconscious Mind as Partners in Action** 155
Stop day dreaming—The "magic power" is within you—You have made yourself ready—You have tested that power—Goals are all-important—Your subconscious in action—First step forward—Then, many steps forward—Nothing can stop you

18 **You and Your Subconscious Mind as Partners in Action . . . in Your Everyday Life** 164
It's a wonderful feeling!—There is much more ahead—What has been good is good today—Practical needs are important—The bright side is important—Self-importance is important—Load up your subconscious!—A red-letter day for you—

Action and accomplishment are "twins"—Opportunities unlimited—Self-influence will grow and prosper

19 **You and Your Subconscious Mind as Partners in Action . . . in Relation to Faith**   173
Blind faith is misleading—True faith opens all doors—Faith is belief in action—Faith in your God—Man is related to a creative plan—Man's faith in man—Keep faith with yourself—Faith induces optimism—Make faith a basic influence— Dynamic faith for you

20 **You and Your Subconscious Mind as Partners in Action . . . in Relation to Knowledge and Learning**   183
Strengthen your life through learning—Knowledge conquers problems—There is just one right answer —Knowledge attracts opportunities—Knowledge and self-influence are good partners—Knowledge is storing up in your subconscious—All positive knowledge you acquire will be used—Go after positive knowledge consistently

21 **You and Your Subconscious Mind as Partners in Action . . . in Relation to Goals in Life**   192
The most important budget in the world!—Do you get value received from what you do?—Budget your life—This way to achievement—Major goals first—Alternate goals are important—Timetables for progress—Never turn back—Variety is necessary—Sell your goals to others—Goals must be hand-made

22 **You and Your Subconscious Mind as Partners in Action . . . in Relation to Success**   201
Success is true romance—Before success—Success

can be made to happen to you—Don't compromise with failure—Not who you are, but what you do—Success is for today

23 **You and Your Subconscious Mind as Partners in Action . . . in Relation to Happiness** 208
Happiness should not be exceptional—What is happiness?—Actions bring happiness—Happiness pays life-long dividends—Make happiness a habit —Happiness is giving—Happiness is seeing right —Happiness is acting positively—Happiness is living your faith—Happiness is harmonious action

24 **You and Your Subconscious Mind as Partners in Action . . . in Relation to Heredity and Environment** 216
Twin influences in your life—Which one governs your life?—The influence of heredity—Many positive inheritances—Heredity factors under control —Self-control is stronger influence—Environmental factors under control—Choose the best of each

25 **You and Your Subconscious Mind as Partners in Action . . . in Relation to Health** 225
Just a shiny penny, not a gold piece—"Even as you and I . . ."—But it wasn't a new penny—Take a lesson from the penny—Some people look bright and shiny—Look right and you must be right— First, take care of your body—Adopt good mental health habits—Provide for spiritual good health— Subconscious support of good health—Look shiny, and mean it!—You look just fine!

26 **You and Your Subconscious Mind as Partners in Action . . . in Relation to Problems** 234
Sympathy doesn't solve problems—Everybody has problems—You can live well with your problems —Concentrate on answers—Handle all problems

*"1-2-3"—Everyone's problems are his own respon-
sibility—Problems answered equal achievement*

27 **You and Your Subconscious Mind as Partners in Action . . . in Relation to Love**   **241**
*You must learn how to love—A conflict between
desire and will—Let yourself go, and love!—What
is love?—Suppressed love is frustrating—Men
need a variety of love—A man needs a woman,
and love—The needs and desires of a woman—
Action brings fulfilled love—Love, and be loved,
through action—There is only one kind of true love*

28 **You and Your Subconscious Mind as Partners in Action . . . in Relation to Security**   **251**
*Security can be guaranteed—Security within and
around you—Take advantage of positive environment—Fight negative forces from within—Inner
security comes from inner strength*

29 **You and Your Subconscious Mind as Partners in
Action . . . in Relation to Creativeness and Self-
Expression**   **257**
*You are a creative being—What's new with you?
Try out your good ideas—Be creative about rela-
tionships—Meet competition with creativeness—
Good ideas often save the day—Produce your
good ideas*

PART 4 | A NEW LIFE

30 **A New Model of You, A More Important Person**   **265**
*Congratulation to a more important person—How
do you compare with that ideal model?—That*

*new, better model is you—The many attributes of
this new model—Keep using subconscious self-influence—Thank you!—Great expectations ahead*

31 A Plan for Living for This New You 270
*You have planned a bright future!—You will al-
ways do these positive things—That promised perfection*

PART 5 | PRACTICE PROJECTS

Page 277 to page 285

INTRODUCTION

How to Make This Book

Work for You

Money and financial security can be yours!
Zestful living and happiness can be yours!
Glowing health and lots of energy can be yours!

• Tell me how!

We have been training men and women in all walks of life for twenty-six years. I have seen miracles happen to wonderful men and women. Miracles will happen to you too—when you start using your Subconscious Power!

• All results are mental in origin!

All of us accept the fundamental principles that progress is mental in origin. It first must have the approval of the mind. Then the Subconscious Power takes over.

The construction of your home was mental in origin. Either in your own mind, or the builder's, or both. Your car and all its modern improvements were mental in origin. The conveniences in your kitchen were mental in origin.

• You control your future

We don't want to wait until something happens—we must make it happen! That is the whole purpose of this book—to make our future to order.

Experiences of thousands of people lead me to believe that most of us want:

1. Money and financial security
2. Happiness and peace of mind
3. Health and zestful energy

I am a firm believer that we can make these goals come true in our personal lives. When we start thinking right—things happen! They have to happen! Powerful fundamental laws are in operation!

• Right thinking and you

When we start thinking right it is easy to put our Subconscious Power to work for us on a 24-hour basis. These laws work with mathematical accuracy. They will work for you, for me, for anyone who will stop long enough to investigate and to go into *planned action*.

Before the laws will work for us, we must become aware! You will become aware as you read the first few chapters of this book. You can't miss! They aren't my laws—they are yours—they belong to those who will stop long enough to think, analyze, and act!

• Why do some people fail?

It is a modern tragedy to see fine people fail to make their plans come true. I see thousands of them every year. From outward appearance they seem to have "everything"—and yet they fail.

People fail because "things" aren't working right on the "inside." When our thinking and feeling are wrong—then we make it absolutely impossible for "things" to work correctly on the "outside." Just a little thinking and investigation will prove this point beyond all doubt.

• Three reasons!

There are three reasons why people aren't fully productive, happy and secure. Think with me now—as I give you these reasons:

1. Negative past experiences. Experiences that hurt—set us back—disappointed us, put questions in our minds about our ability—our future. Many of our lives are filled with negative experiences. Experiences that have been forgotten to the conscious mind—but are still exacting their toll in indecisions, in lack of confidence, and in uncertainty.

These negative pictures—this stream of negative thinking and therefore action—can be changed. You can change it! This book will guide you in that change!

2. **Lack of direction.** Many wonderful people have lots of energy, ambition and drive but poor direction! Our lives become confused. Sometimes they look and feel like a mental junk shop.

As you read and study *Your Subconscious Power*—design, definite purpose and an all-consuming plan will come into your life. When we turn the searchlight of thinking and analysis "inside" with an outside objectivity—you just can't miss.

3. **Poor human relations.** Failure to understand people and get them to like us and boost us—this invariably robs success and happiness from our lives. We let people mix us up—discourage us—talk us out of action and results which might have been infinitely rewarding.

In this book, readers, we will carefully lay the ground work for complete understanding in Human Relations, as we make Your Subconscious Power work for you!

• The "facts of life" are mysteries to most people

For most people, things are always happening which they don't want to happen—causing fear, tension, anxiety. For these same people, the good things they want to happen seldom do— such as enough money, real love, achievement and recognition. For them, life is like a series of nightmares, and many take desperate means to escape them. Unfortunately, these people are running the wrong way—into the darkness where the "facts of life" are mysteries. To make sure you are facing in the right direction, this book begins with the revelation of facts about life you must know, if you are to use your subconscious power effectively.

• People you know

Among the people you know, a few stand out prominently because they have made a success of getting what they want out of life. They are outstanding in business, in the professions, in their home life, and in leading stimulating, adventuresome lives. They are fine people—but are they any better than you? Are they more deserving—or endowed with something special? NO, on both counts! They are getting what they want because they consider themselves important enough to have only the best in life. Chapter 2 shows you how to establish yourself as one of these outstanding people.

• Every move you make is the result of powerful influence

It has always been this way, and always will be this way. You do nothing accidentally. You are directed to make every move—both night and day. Even when you are asleep, you are under the spell. Your emotions—your physical actions—your mental efforts—even the value of spiritual effects, are all dominated by the power of influence. Sometimes it pulls against you—sometimes with you. You can't escape influence. What you can do about it, following the lead of outstanding people, is explained in Chapter 3.

• Who is pulling the strings in your life?

This Nation of ours is full of live puppets. They are the people who are completely influenced by others—by negative environment—and by what they call "force of circumstances." They seldom make a move of their own choice. You can see them all around you, at any time, plodding through life on a leash. They even have themselves believing that somebody should always pull the strings in life. Here's where the book gets down to cases about *you*. If there are strings on your life, in somebody else's hands, now is the time to shake them off. Chapters 4 and 5 show you how to do this, and how to pull your own strings. This reveals an insight into your subconscious power!

• The "opium" of normal living

People living puppet-like lives are in the majority. The usual standard of living is "to get along as best I can" (with somebody or something more dominating pulling the strings)—and "to hope for the best" (meaning: hoping somebody will pull the right string, sometime). Since this is the way it is with the majority, it is the "normal" way of life. As a consequence, this business of being "normal" is highly over-rated. Normal living is like smoking opium—the wonderful things are all dreams! You can't get what you want—do what you want—be what you want—living "normally." You must live abnormally—and through the power of your subconscious, you will live away above normal!

• You can't live normally and live happily

Normal living puts restrictions on high emotional experiences —and even on high spiritual experiences. It has established all kinds of taboos on love, affection, making friends—and on doing anything unusual. Normal living puts a premium on happiness—makes people expect real happiness to come rarely. This is the wrong way to live! The Creator intends us to use our emotional capacities—to love and be adventurous—not subdue them. Through subconscious power you will find the freedom to live happily—above normal!

• You can't live normally and be successful

The code of "normal" living is one of "have not"—or "have little." That is just the opposite of success, isn't it? And among the normal livers there is that widespread disease of daydreaming and wishing for a better life. Certainly this isn't the way to have success. Not a single successful person you know, or who you have heard about or read about, believes in normal living. The fact is that normal living and success just don't go together! To help you step up to above normal living is the reason Chapters 6 and 7 were written.

• No one possesses greater power than is within you

There is no denying that above-normal living calls for more positive output than does normal living. It does *not* take more energy—more work—or more time. It takes time and energy just to walk a treadmill through life. Above-normal living calls for directed energy—directed effort—directed use of time. The only one who can successfully direct your life is yourself! The power to direct yourself wherever you want to go in life is within you. It is in your subconscious mind. And no one— absolutely no one—possesses this power to a greater degree than you do!

• Power you can't turn off

The power of your subconscious is subject to control—but there is one thing you can't do about it. You can't turn it off! It is working and influencing you every minute of every day, and every minute of every night. You can stop physical activity —say to yourself, "I am going to do nothing"—or even go to sleep. Do "nothing" or do "anything," and your subconscious mind keeps on being active. It is a tireless, never-ceasing power —and it is within you! The important factor is that it is a power—a power that acts on you constantly. You can control that power, instead of letting it go to waste. Get to know what this power really is, and what it can do for you, as described in Chapter 8.

• Control this power and you control life itself

Control the power of your suconscious mind and you have positive control over your own life! It is the control center of influence—and you should not let it be controlled by outside, distracting influences. Read Chapter 9 and learn the secrets of this intimate, inner power of yours. Learn here what it does and how it can help you accomplish what has seemed like the "impossible" in the past.

• Build your own "Garden of Eden"

There isn't a person who hasn't dreamed of some kind of an ideal existence—of life in a "Garden of Eden," or in a Shangrila. These are like the dreams you have had of a life where everything was perfect. This you should know: if you will make such dreams definite enough, and bring the power of your subconscious mind to bear on them, you can create your own "Garden of Eden," where you can live for the rest of your life! Chapter 10 points the way!

• Daydreams waste this power

If you just daydream about that ideal life, and then let yourself be dragged back into the reality of "normal" living, you are creating a purgatory for yourself. When you daydream because it is pleasant escape from reality, you are wasting the power of your subconscious. Your subconscious wants to see those dreams come true. It has the power to make them come true. When you do not exercise that power, either because you don't know how or because you imagine dreams can't really come true, you are letting that vital energy go to waste. The power is there! It's up to you!

• You can't afford to waste a minute of your precious life

How many minutes do you have left to live? You can't be sure of the number, but it runs up into the millions. But if you did know how many more minutes were allotted to you, each one would become most precious. You wouldn't waste a single one! The minutes are no less precious because you have so many to look forward to. Every one is loaded with opportunity, and you can't afford to waste opportunity. And you don't have to. Your subconscious works every minute of every day, and if you use its power correctly, every minute will count for good in your life. Chapter 11 tells you the positive truths about dreams and precious minutes, and how they relate to your subconscious.

• A science everybody can master

Is the use and control of subconscious power a science? It is! It is founded on knowledge and research that has been accumulating for generations. It has its roots in the sciences of medicine, psychiatry, psychology, and human relations. Its application, however, is personal and intimate with each individual. All it takes to apply this science to your own life, under your own guidance, is understanding of the basic principles. These are easy to understand because they make sense, and because you can see the results for yourself. All the details are in Chapter 12.

• Put yourself on the pedestal of success

There is no better way to describe the effects of the proper use of the power of your subconscious than to say that it makes a success out of life. This is true because this power can be kept on the positive side always. When this power is guiding everything you do, you are always up there on the pedestal of success. Read Chapter 13 on how to use this power this way. Learn how it works even while you sleep. Learn how to create that wonderful state of positively influenced conditioned sleep as soon as possible.

• The influence that shaped your past

If you were to write your autobiography, you would have difficulty describing why a lot of things happened in your life. All you could say is that "this" or "that" happened—but you don't know why. It's too late to change any of your past, of course. But if things don't change in your life today, the story of your future could sound just like the story of your past. Why things happened as they did was because more negative than positive influences were working on you. The subconscious was responsible for both. Certainly this points to the absolute need for controlling your subconscious. The person who knows why things happen as they do is a strong individual. Learn the "why" about your own life through Chapters 14 and 15 and how, by exercising this control, your life will start improving now.

• Your subconscious power can shape a brilliant future

Under your own control, both while you are awake and asleep, your subconscious power will take you forward into a stimulating, rewarding future. You can even predict your future and know it will be as you want it to be! See your future this way, in Chapter 16.

• Second best is impossible for you when this power is used

Once you turn on the power of your subconscious mind, under your own control, you will stop living "normally." Second-best, come-what-may mediocrity all will be forgotten effects in your life. The reason is that your subconscious power will put you into action—doing all the things that add up to your idea of an ideal life. Your subconscious power will keep you doing only those things. It will become your willing partner—both day and night—as you will find described in Chapter 17.

• No limit to what subconscious power can do for you

You cannot overwork this power. In fact the more you use it positively, the better it will serve. There is no special time to use it this way. It is there to be used every day. It should be as much a part of your everyday life as is waking, sleeping, eating. It is a perfectly natural force—adapting itself to every need and desire you have. Chapter 18 explains its limitless possibilities in your everyday life.

• The source of peace of mind

Those who have that understanding of the spiritual forces that bring comforting faith into their lives are depending on subconscious power. Faith must be within a person. It lives in the subconscious. Those who have knowledge that serves them positively, are also depending on the subconscious power within them—and they act accordingly. Peace of mind comes from faith, understanding and knowledge that are centered in the subconscious. The key to this inner strength, which can be *yours* through subconscious power, is revealed in Chapter 19 and Chapter 20.

● The source of unlimited energy

The subconscious is the master motivator. Under control, and directed by you, it will eliminate fatigue, drabness, and desire to put things off until "tomorrow." It will put all goals within your reach—and take you to them unswervingly. The keys to this unlimited energy are handed you in Chapters 21 and 22.

● The power that keeps you right with the world

The state of your physical, mental, emotional and spiritual health is of constant concern to you, of course. If any one of these is off center, it makes the world look wrong. To most folks, it seems almost impossible to keep all four in balance all the time. Consequently life is a bit rough most of the time. It doesn't have to be this way. Read Chapters 23, 24 and 25, on how to use your subconscious power to keep you always right with the world—and yourself!

● Convert problems to achievements

No matter what you may have been told, you can't eliminate problems from your life. You are going to have them always—

even in that ideal existence. But you can convert problems to action that results in achievement—through your subconscious power. "How" is in Chapter 26.

• The way to fulfilled love

Half-way love is no love at all, simply because if love is subdued or diluted by restraint, it is not satisfying. Love is an urge that should not be subdued. Love fully expressed and demonstrated stimulates the whole life of a person. The expression of love is a strong factor with subconscious power. It will take you all the way to fulfillment—as described in the "how to do it" Chapter 27.

• Money is made in your mind through this power

The money that you need in your life is not the paycheck or minimum income that just lets you "get by." The money you really need are those amounts you can exchange for the things you want, above and beyond just getting by. You need money for those "extras" you deserve—for real security—for growth. Your subconscious has the power to make all those things so important to you, that getting the money for them becomes a certain, positive action. With your subconscious, the bigger the picture you set up there first, the bigger the end results will certainly be. The sure way to real and satisfying security is told in Chapter 28.

• The power that brings infinite rewards in life

There are many things you have an unusual talent for. You have a variety of abilities. You are productive of many good ideas. In other words, you have the potential ability to be creative in many ways—and yet you are using few of them. Through subconscious power, you can unleash all of your talents and abilities—and reap the rewards of a full life. See Chapter 29 for the recipe.

• Turn on the power and really live

Turn on your subconscious power! It is the answer to the only kind of life really worth living. The results if you turn on your subconscious power? See for yourself, in Chapters 30 and 31. There's a new model of you displayed there that is ready for immediate delivery!

PART ONE

YOUR PLAN

1

What Is Life?

ONE MAN CLIMBS THE "LADDER OF SUCCESS" AS IF BY magic, in apparently predetermined steps. Another fumbles, slips, and is apparently pushed back as though bedeviled by "black magic."

Why? Every person wants to make progress in life. Some do, some do not. Why?

There is an undeniable answer to "why"!

One woman typifies graciousness and happiness in her role of wife, mother and home executive, as though her "cup runneth over." Another in the same role appears burdened, unblest, unduly time-worn.

Why? Fulfillment reaches its climax in a woman in this role. Yet it fits some and apparently not others. Why?

There is an unqualified answer to "why."

One person exemplifies faith in his life, faith in others, faith in himself or herself, faith in the future. Another wears "doubt" like a badge-of-office in life, apparently finding it difficult to trust much of anything.

Why? Faith is a far more comfortable factor to live with than doubt. Yet faith appears to bless some and elude others. Why?

There is an indisputable answer to "why"!

• Is life a question mark?

"Why? Why others, and not me?" This is the eternal question mark in the lives of so many people who despair of finding success, love, security, recognition. There's a certain answer to "why"!

"Why? Why am I singled out, among all others?" This is the plaguing question of so many persons who face unanswered problems, tensions, uncertainties. There's the same, solid answer here to "why"!

There is the same ultimate answer to every "why" about every person's pattern of life, whether he has an illustrious biography to his credit or whether "life has been a mystery" to him.

The ultimate answer to why life is good or not good is centered on the control or lack of control of a power that is possessed by everyone. Control of this power brings results as if "by magic." Lack of control of this power brings results that cloud a person's life like "black magic."

This is the power of your subconscious mind. This power exerts a continuous influence over your life, a dominating influence that is in force 24 hours a day! When you lack control over it, it can take you on an unpredictable, "take-a-chance" course through life. When you do control it, it will guide you unerringly along a predetermined course, a course of your own choosing.

Have you ever peered into the "looking glass" of human existence and seen the image of yourself there, and asked, "What is life? What is my life?" A thoughtful observation on this "image" of you would show that life—your life—is a "reflection" of action. Your life is an exact image of what you *do* and what happens to you.

Twenty-four hours a day, your life is a combination of physical, intellectual, emotional and spiritual action. Even while you sleep, there is physical action in the refreshment of your body. There is often emotional action, as well.

• This is your life

If you could look in back of that mirror of your life, you would find that everything you do and everything that happens to you is caused by some influence. For every minute of every 24 hours, some influence is motivating every one of your actions. These actions say about you: "This is my life!"

A straightforward way to describe your life as it has been, and as it is today, would be for you to ask and answer this question about yourself: "How much of this influence do I control and how much of it is uncontrolled in my life?" The answer to this question would also answer every puzzling "Why?" that exists for you.

• Let your subconscious have control

The achievement of a full life, and the claiming of your share of the world-full of opportunities that surround you, depend upon the *balance of control* of influence being in your hands, consistently. The key to this positive self-control is the power of your subconscious mind, with its power under your direct control.

Two kinds of influence are shaping your life. One is "outside" influence, which so often seems to stand like a dominating giant over you. "Outside" influence always seems to be exerting pressure on your will, forcing you to do things, or to cause things to happen to you, simply because such influence seems to be too big for you to resist.

The other kind is "inner" influence, that of the power of your subconscious. This is a dynamic power which is never turned off. But if you did not know the secret of this power, you would be inclined to say that your subconscious is eccentric because it can "go along" with "outside" influence. At such times, if your subconscious could speak, it would say: "Apparently my master wants to act this way, so I'll support that action." Enough of this kind of subconsciously supported action results in fears, big problems made out of little ones and bigger "Whys?" than ever before.

• Choose a new life

But there is another brilliant, sparkling side to subconscious influence. When it is under control by you, it will successfully combat negative "outside" influences. It will help you to pick the best from "outside" and to discard the rest. It will establish its own positive pattern of influence that will be bigger than any other influence in your life. Since such control allows you to predetermine what this influence will be, you can choose the pattern of action in your life. A more brilliant, sparkling reflection will then appear in the "mirror of life" for you, to which you can proudly point and say, "This is now my life!"

Your subconscious mind is like an ever-running mountain stream. Uncontrolled, and running free down the mountainside, the stream rushes along pell-mell, apparently intent only on "keeping running." But it is not quite free-running. Boulders in the stream-bed disturb its course, and cause it to foam up in a show of power; still, the obstruction remains, and the power goes for nothing. A mountain spur forces the stream to deviate from a straight course. In a show of power, it tries to dig into this obstruction, but still it has to detour. In a like manner, your *uncontrolled* subconscious mind-power expends itself to little desirable avail in your life. The "boulders" of fear and the "obstructions" of uncertainty tend to consume its only apparent power.

• Your subconscious is a source of power

But, under control, your subconscious, like the mountain stream, presents a remarkably different picture. The mountain stream under control with dams, pipelines, generators produces useful, productive power under control. The water itself hasn't changed, nor is the source of this controlled power any different. The controlled power still comes from the water in action. The same is true with your subconscious. Under your control, its power becomes useful and productive in your life. The skill of such control might be likened to the building of those controlling elements on the stream. Just as certainly as such things can be built by man, the skill of positive self-influence can be learned by man, by you. As with the water, your subconscious mind itself will be no different, and the source of power will be the same. The source of the power of "inner" influence is your subconscious mind in action, no matter how the power is used. The difference in its value lies entirely in the degree of control.

• Life is influenced action

What is life? Life is a "reflection" of action that is governed by the ever-present power of influence. The power of "inner" influence can be the greatest arm of strength in your life, under control. The control of the power of your subconscious so that the major influences in your life are positive, progressive and predictable *starts* with you and *ends* with you. This has always been so, and it always will be so.

You are about to "tell" your subconscious: "This is the kind of a life I want." The power of your subconscious mind will be directed toward that goal, and it will be achieved. Because you are about to take control, you are the most important person in the world!

In a moment, I will prove that to you!

IN SUM

You can choose your own kind of life. But, first, you must bridle your subconscious. Make it work for you.

---

o→   **RESULT-GETTING PROJECTS**   ←o

Come to terms with your understanding of influence in your life, by verifying its powerful presence. You will need a piece of paper and a pencil for this. You are going to produce a most revealing picture of "what life is" . . . for yourself. Not a moment of the time you put in on these projects will have "momentary" value. The results will have lasting value as you go on with the book. For your own sake, don't make this a "mental exercise." Do use the paper and pencil! First draw a line down the center of the paper, from top to bottom. Head the left-hand column "Outside influence" . . . and the right-hand column "My own influence." Now the projects:

1. Review everything that you did during the last 24 hours. Briefly list each action under either of the column headings. For example: you went to work, or did some shopping, read a book, had some fun. Which of the actions came about purely because of your own choice and deci-

sion (listed under "My own influence"); which happened because you had to do something, because of "outside influence"? List everything you can recall doing.

2. Review what you did during the last week. Briefly list the things you did that had lasting effects, such as becoming chairman of a committee, or being part of some unusual activity. Put them down under the proper "Influence" headings.

3. Review your life, up to this moment. Consider the most significant factors in (a) your vocational life; (b) your family life; (c) your social life. Listing them in that a-b-c order, determine whether each has come about through your own influence or through outside influence. For example, what is the major influence that put you in your present status in your work, and is it the result of "inner" or "outer" influence?

4. Envision the week immediately ahead. Consider one or two out-of-the-ordinary actions you are pretty sure you will be part of. Again, this can be in relation to your vocational, family or social life. Determine whether this forecast of a "piece of your future" is the result of your own influence, or outside influence. So list them on the paper.

Now, what do you have? You have a word picture of action in your life. This means that this is your life. You have a true picture of the effect of influence. But, most of all, you have a true picture of how the scales balance between action due to your own influence on yourself and action due to outside influence. Frankly recognizing and accepting this picture of your life is a noteworthy preparatory step in putting the "balance of control" in your own hands. You are better prepared to direct the power of your subconscious toward the right action.

(*Don't throw your list away! For safe-keeping for future reference, leave it as a bookmark at this chapter!*)

2

You Are the Most Important Person in the World

This book is all about me, ———————————————,
the most important person in the world!

IF YOU WILL WRITE YOUR NAME IN THAT SPACE AFTER "me," you will be putting the finishing touch on this book that I want it to have. This book is written with you as the main character. This name identification is necessary to make it a finished piece of work. So, will you accommodate me, please, by putting your name in its proper place?

Perhaps you hesitate, because you feel that this would be a display of extreme egotism. With what you feel is appropriate humility, you might want to say: "I wouldn't want to let other people think that I considered myself the most important person in the world!"

10

• "I . . . My . . . Me!"

I can understand this reaction, because I know that you have had uncomfortable associations with people for whom the most important words in the language are "*I . . . my . . .* and *me.*" You have known people who appear to be intoxicated with a sense of self-importance. You don't want to be classified with either, and for this you are to be commended. Yet I am asking you to emphasize "me" and "important," and to do so more or less publicly by writing your name in this book.

A paradox? No, not at all! But it could be pointing up a different viewpoint than you have ever had about yourself. This is my viewpoint of you, as I write, and it should be yours. As far back in time as you can remember, you have had the desire to act as though you were the most important person to yourself. Yet you have been influenced by that code of undue humility, and you have probably suppressed that desire. But this you should not have done!

• Humbleness is unbecoming

Modesty is a cloak of superior material which you should wear on proper occasions, when it will become you. But if you wear it as an everyday vestment, it will become shabby and threadbare. And threadbare modesty turns into the cast-off raiment of humbleness. This is not the proper dress for you, because if you style yourself as being humble, you are relegating yourself to an unimportant status. You are identifying yourself with that undesirable caste of "little" people.

I do not envision you, as the main character in this book, as a "little" person. I envision you as a person who exemplifies the "dignity of mankind." I envision you as a self-respecting person, deserving of the recognition and status that both your Creator and the society of men intended you to have, and which your closest associates want you to have. I envision you as a person with all of the potential power to create the best kind of a life for yourself.

I believe that there is intrinsic truth in this characterization. I believe that if you and I were having a confidential chat, you would tell me that this is a standard of self-identification that has always been your most intimate aspiration.

• The creator made you different

Your life is surrounded by logical manifestations of your right to this important status. One of these is inherent in your birthright: your Creator made you a *distinctive* person with a distinctive purpose in life. Whatever your academic interpretation of the Supreme Being is, I know that it includes faith in His creative plan. In His plan, no human is made inconsequential or without a purpose in life. On the other hand, He endows each person with the *will to live* according to his or her own distinctiveness. Only when this will is coupled with purposeful action, does a person's individuality have meaning. Therefore, in the eyes of the Creator, you are living according to *His* will for you when you put importance upon your individuality.

• Being important is your right

Another logical demonstration of your right to this important status came at a time when you *acted* upon some basic belief of yours. For example, this might have been an action that supported a friend at a time when he needed the strength that came from your interest in him. You believed he was right and you believed in him. This element of distinctive belief could come only from you, and it resulted in a contribution to the life of your friend, to yourself. The will to act this way was an endowment of the Creator, and the action you took fulfilled a basic purpose of your life. And at that moment, you were the most important person in the world, to your friend!

Furthermore, you have notable status in the material, tangible scheme of things. Our society, in its long "trial-and-error" development, has learned one cardinal fact. This is that society can have hope of perfection only when the welfare of each individual member is at its highest, most desirable level.

Actually this society of ours has a great big ego at the core of it. It's a positive, even an aggressive, ego and we shouldn't be ashamed of it. In fact, your importance is dependent upon your own ego being directly related to this big "master ego." Successful, happy people who have already learned this secret want others to join them. They believe in "the-more-the-merrier." That's logical because, if your material welfare is on a high plane, it will help boost up the general welfare of others. But if you hold back, or drag your feet, you are pulling the average down! This is a case of one ego supporting another in a frank, unabashed manner.

Either way, therefore, you are most important. You are negatively important if you do not put in with the "progressive party" in life, but you are positively important if you act according to your rightful status.

• Satisfy your inner urges

Still another proof of your importance lies in emotional relationships with others. Everyone is alike in having some fundamental urges. These are the urges for recognition, prestige, and self-expression, and for love, good-will and friendship. Yet none of these urges can be satisfied by individuals alone. Such satisfaction requires emotional relationships with others. This is so because no one can really have recognition, or love, or friendship without also giving them to others. Therefore, you are part of an emotional relationship with others. When any of those urges are satisfied, you are the most important person in the world. Every time you give and you receive in such a relationship, you are substantiating your own importance.

• No one is more important than you

Then, finally, there is that outstanding and most logical angle of self-importance. This is the matter of your importance to yourself. A common tendency is for people to say: "Oh well, it goes without saying that I am important to myself." If YOU have this tendency, I want you to imagine that you are looking me straight in the eye as I say to you, it doesn't "go without saying!" And, particularly, it won't do to have that attitude *here*. I am vitally concerned with your having a *different* kind of an attitude before you get any further into this book.

You will go on reading this book with one of two attitudes affecting your reaction to it. You will read it with a feeling that there are a lot of good ideas expressed, which could be applied to lots of other people. But for YOU, you might feel, it's "maybe," or *"mañana,"* or "I should try them." If this were your attitude, it would "go without saying" that you don't put much importance on yourself.

Or, you will read the book impelled by the feeling that it is written for you simply because it is written for the most important people. You know, however, that you can't cash in on the reactions of others. The value of the contents of this book starts and ends with you. Are you important to yourself? Then demonstrate it, by signing your name as I have suggested!

• Your name packs power

Is this name-signing just a clever gesture? No, not at all! It is the first concrete step in a series of stimulating, powerfully practical experiences that will be yours, provided you think yourself important enough to be part of them. Signing your name at this chapter heading will cause a chain reaction in your life, because it will result in a manifestation of the power of your subconscious mind.

Is this book all about you? When you sign your name, you are saying, "yes, I believe it is!"

Are you the most important person in the world? When you sign your name you are saying: "yes, I believe I am, in relation to a role in life that will best exemplify my distinctiveness."

These are unusual, perhaps remarkable, statements for you to put your name to. Once you have put that singular brand of yours on them, they will color every sentence you read. This coloring, this personal slant, will be the result of the work of your subconscious mind.

This, then, will be "just another book," or it will be a personal treatise, depending upon whether you let your subconscious put that "coloring" on it. But the choice is yours. How important are you to yourself? Important enough to sign your name, now?

• Be influenced the positive way

There is a powerful symbolism in this act of signing your name. Your name was given you as a mark of individual identification. But, more significantly, it is a mark of your individual importance. Since the moment it was bestowed upon you, you have been subject to a major force that has made this individual "you" have an important or unimportant status. This force is influence. When you sign your name to that statement, you are inviting a positive influence to affect the importance of that name. This positive influence will be abetted by the work of your subconscious mind. You are about to participate in a demonstration which will display the power of your subconscious.

When you have finished this chapter, and after you have signed your name, close the book. Place it in a conspicuous spot and go about some normal activity. To make this demonstration doubly effective, do something that is normally quite absorbing to you. Work in the garden, read the paper, even look at TV. But keep the closed book in a spot where you can see it.

Two things will happen to you during this period. Both will appear to be involuntary reactions. First, you won't be able to keep your thoughts from the fact that you signed your name to that statement. You will think about what an unpredicted action that was, saying that this book is all about yourself and that you are so important. At the moment, you won't be able to resolve much from this conjecture, except that it was most unusual, for you! (I assure you that a bigger answer will come later!)

Secondly, you will feel some of the thoughts expressed in these two chapters bouncing around in your mind. You will begin to wonder if it isn't time for a change, time to be more concerned about what you are doing with your life. For the moment, you won't be able to resolve these questions, either. But these answers, too, *will* come later.

Actually, neither of these reactions will be "involuntary." They will come as the result of the influence of your subconscious mind, which has been stimulated by that impressive action you took in signing your name.

• Subconscious power in action!

If you think you are important enough to yourself to call upon the power of your subconscious to work positively for you, then make this demonstration. It will verify your belief in your importance in life. This is most important to both of us, because, in writing this book, I envision you with this belief.

After you have made this demonstration, and you have felt

the power of its influence, go on with your book. You will be properly conditioned for what is ahead, not with the inferior attitude of a person who is afraid to demonstrate and declare his importance, but with the attitude of a person who is about to have his superior status confirmed.

IN SUM

You, as the most important person in the world, have a purpose in life.

Do not underestimate its importance.

---

o→   RESULT-GETTING PROJECTS   ←o

Reinforce your elevation to this status of importance by making the following agreements with yourself:

1. *To demonstrate the importance of your beliefs to your-self, and to the world about you.* Within the next 24 hours, demonstrate your belief in something or someone by deliberately acting in support of that belief. For example, display your belief in your religion by some positive act. Here and now, make an agreement with yourself to (write in your choice of action) _____

_____.

2. *To demonstrate your importance in what the world offers in the matter of tangible, material things.* Within the next 24 hours, take at least the first steps in associating

yourself with some progressive action, something which symbolizes "going forward" in life. It can be the joining of a charitable or civic organization. Here and now, make an agreement with yourself to (write in the progressive action of your choice) _____.

3. *To demonstrate your importance in relationship to others.* Within the next 24 hours, make a deliberate effort to render a service to someone, a family member, friend or vocational associate. Right now, make an agreement with yourself to (define the service you will render) _____
_____.

Each one of these projects, in addition to the act of signing your name, will cause the power of your subconscious to be a positive influence in your life. Each one will serve to confirm your distinctiveness. In each case, at the moment you act in accordance with those agreements, you are the "most important person in the world" to others related to that action. These actions point up your importance. But even more than that, these actions will demonstrate that you can be important all the time, since you can act and re-act in a similar manner, time and time again. Just now they will reinforce the toe-hold you have made on a stimulating, new kind of a life.

3

The Dynamic Factor which Master-Controls Your Life

WATCH OUT FOR THE NEXT FEW MOMENTS! THEY ARE loaded with a power that is going to take complete control of your life!

Within these next few moments, something is going to stick a needle into you and cause you to *jump into action,* or something is going to cinch you to a standstill and leave you like a helplessly tied victim of circumstances!

You can't stop the clock! It's ticking off the moments like a referee and, at the "count of ten," you are either going to "get up and go" or you are going to be counted out. Whichever happens to you, you can give credit or blame to that power, because you will act just the way it directs you to act. This power will dominate you just as certainly as you are reading these words.

But this is not the first time this has happened to you, nor will it be the last time. Your whole life has already been dominated by this controlling power, and if you live another hundred years, every single day will be controlled by this same power.

If you have not been warned about this power before, keep your eyes open and your mind alert, especially in the next few moments. You will be able to "see" and "feel" it taking control, because the stage has been set for a demonstration of it in your own life. Become *aware* of that stage setting, because it shows something else about this power. It indicates that you can control this "power" in your life. The stage was set in the last chapter, when I said that this book was written about you. Do you believe that?

• Applaud yourself

You do believe this book was written about you if your name has been impressively inscribed in it, and if you made those three agreements with yourself! You have the feeling that you have done something worthwhile. Even before you have gone into action, you feel good about yourself. You feel like something is "applauding" inside of you. And something is! It is self-rightness, self-respect. It is just the opposite of conscience, which shakes its head in disapproval of your intentions.

When you signed your name, and made those agreements, you caused your subconscious to build up a positive influence in your life. Since this positive build-up came from the suggestions made to you, is this not evidence that the book is written for you? Every chapter is written with the same objective, to cause something positive to happen to you. What you have just done is meant to be the first step in cultivating a habit that is important to you in this book about you. This is the habit of participation, of "getting into the act" with me, when I suggest it.

- **Part of your life is in this book**

There is life in this book, the elements of a dynamic life. The very nature of its contents calls for your participation. So, I am continuing with the assumption that you are a participant. This is not going to be a very impressive "drama of life" if the main character is sitting on the sidelines! So if you haven't gotten "into character," stop here, go back and sign that statement of importance and get started on those agreements. Let these acts become the positive influence they should be in your life. Feel that "applause" from within. Then we can go on with a good understanding of your story!

In the actions you took in stepping up to this important position of self-rightness and self-respect, there was a dynamic force at work. This was a power that worked ON you and within you. This was the force that patterned those "agreements." This was the power that caused those emotional and intellectual reactions you had and which you still have.

- **What is really controlling your life**

The name of this power is used rather glibly in the everyday language of most people, yet it is something that should have our profoundest respect. And when we analyze some of its effects, we could say that we should hold it in awe. This force that worked on and within you, in those actions, is influence, and influence is the dynamic factor that master-controls your life and the life of everyone else!

There never has been a moment, and there never will be a moment, in your life when you are not affected by this power. It affects you when you are at your best, and when you are at a low ebb. It affects you when you are with people, and when you are alone. It affects you when you are in dynamic action,

and when you are "doing nothing." It even affects you while
you sleep. Every minute of every day of your life is controlled
by this master force we call influence!

• Don't be a living puppet

If I wanted to indulge in a bit of "fantasy fiction" here, I
could paint a picture of influence as a "master," making puppets
of all of us. I could picture you with a lot of strings attached to
your body, with you doing whatever that puppet-master
influence made you do. But I can't imagine you in the role of a
puppet, although you and I both know people who could assume this role. These are people who have let themselves
become captives of uncontrolled influence. They are people
who have let themselves be humbled into puppet status by not
considering themselves important enough for anything other
than come-what-may influence. Many such persons have become slaves of uncontrolled influence because, at first, they
thought it would be easier that way only to find that the "easier
way" was an illusion.

But a while ago, you painted a more realistic picture of you
and influence. In Chapter 1, you took an inventory of some
of the effects of influence in your life. Take another look at that
book-marked inventory and let us see what it reveals. Everything listed there, of course, is related to action. A bit of analysis will show that there are four areas of action indicated on
that list and in your life. These are the areas of physical action,
emotional action, intellectual action and spiritual action. Of
course, all are not as outward and obvious as physical action,
but you are a party to one or more of those actions continuously.

• You can achieve positive results

Your inventory of influence also revealed something else,
quite dramatically. Those actions that came about, or are fore-

cast, and that are the result of your own desire and decision, were the best actions, for the most part. And you find that if you had used your own influence with greater determination, you could have changed or amended some of those outside influences, to your benefit. This is so because you really know what you want to do and what is best for you. So now you know that in addition to having the scales balanced in favor of action from your own influence, you need to keep your own influence consistently on the positive side.

Yes, influence does master-control your life, but you can become the skilled technician who *controls* most of the influences in your life. In the last chapter, you probed the world of self-influence. Now go all the way, and have a controlled experience, by *going into action* on those three agreements. This can be the beginning of a golden era in your life, through self-influence!

• Depend on yourself first

At this point, you may have some questions. Other people do when I have taken them this far in a developmental experience with self-influence. They have asked: "Can I depend on this self-influence plan to work all the time? Do you mean that I should go out on my own, and figure that I can always call the shots right? What about self-influence in relation to the big things in my life?"

If you have such an inquiring attitude, it is good, because it means that you are alert and you want to know "what and why." It means that you are seeking understanding, with an open mind, you are going to find it.

You can rely upon the effectiveness of self-influence 24 hours a day! Even though you are envisioning a 24-hour period as including such things as eating, driving a car, recreation, and, of all things, sleeping, I repeat, you can use self-influence at all times! As we move along, I'll show you how to use it in every specific circumstance, even while you are sleeping!

But just now, let's cover that question about the "big things."

• Everything you do is important

Nothing you ever do that is of your own volition is a "little thing." Everything that you do that is self-influenced is important at its source, and that source is the most important you! Your job, your home life, your future are all big things in your life, of course. But your active relationship to them is based upon many actions. No one big action is going to make or break your job status or your future. On the other hand, everything you do, even though at times it seems like a "little thing," is affecting one or more of the big things in your life. Self-control of more and more of every action will assure good outcomes in the big things. This is, of course, only common-sense psychology, and that is the basis for all of the contents of this book of yours.

Now about that question, "Will I always call the shots right?" You are not being handed a "genie's lamp" through self-influence. Of course you won't have a 100 per cent score, all the time! But let me ask you a question. What is your score in life right now, where outside influence is calling most of the shots? I know what your answer is. The score isn't anything you are too happy about. You know you could better the score if you could call more of the shots yourself! Through controlled self-influence, you will run up a consistently higher score, and that is our objective!

Suppose you do call a shot wrong once in a while. In the past you might have said: "Well, I have nobody to blame but myself." But in the future, guided by your high standard of importance to yourself, you are going to say: "Well! I learned something I didn't know before. I'll take better aim and try another shot!" As we go along, I am going to show you how to always have that positive attitude, on your own!

• Science has paved the way

You are not a pioneer in this experience with self-influence, you know. It may be a first experience for you, but you are travelling a trail that has already been clearly blazed. Ahead of you have travelled men and women who have used self-influence through all of the ages of recorded history. And immediately ahead of you have travelled the men and women of modern science, the science of human behavior and relationships. The "trial-and-error" experiences of the first group have been evaluated and tested by the second group. Out of this research has come the modern-day knowledge that makes up your book.

Researchers and scholars have always been intrigued by the question: "Why are some people so successful in life, while others are not, when the basic circumstances of both are the same?" Of course, the "man-in-the-street," including you and me, has been mightily intrigued by it, too! The proven answer is that only self-influenced people lead the most successful lives. This has always been so. How they do it is the theme of this, your book.

• The best people are self-influenced

Who are some of the people who have travelled, and *are* travelling, this trail of self-influence? They are all people with high standards of their importance to themselves—just like you. Incidentally, you will observe a common thread running through their lives which acknowledges an overtone of influence that I am sure you and I agree upon. This is the influence of the spirit of their Creator. The hand of the Supreme Being seems to rest encouragingly on the shoulders of these self-influenced people.

Seven centuries before the birth of Christ, the prophet Isaiah had to rely on self-influence to give him strength to fulfill his destiny. In the face of violent opposition, he had to make a strong pact with himself before he could publicly say: "Hear the word of the Lord, ye rulers of Sodom; give ear to the law of our God, you people of Gomorrah."

George Washington, leading his people in a struggle for what they felt was right, had no stable government to back him. In almost every circumstance that called for decision on his part, he had no precedent to guide him. He had to depend upon self-influence. Our country was founded upon the standards of this self-influenced man.

• Leaders are self-influenced

Benjamin Franklin, an apparently versatile genius, living at a time when his people needed his influence, was acting almost 100 per cent on the self-influence principle of living.

Abraham Lincoln, created the leader of a confused people by time and circumstance, brought a new concept of living to his country, by depending and acting upon self-influence.

Clara Barton, seeing a realistic need that could be met only by service, had to back her determination to render this service, with self-influence. Few saw her vision, at first, but the Red Cross was born of the self-influence action of this woman.

Herbert Hoover, world citizen and President of the United States, faced the devastation of an election defeat at the height of his career. He had no one else but himself to turn to. But, long before, Herbert Hoover had learned the value of self-influence, and he used it again, to rise to even greater heights in human accomplishment.

The doctor upon whom you depend to administer to you in

the care of that complex machine that is your body does so in a successful manner only because he combines knowledge and skill with the use of good judgment. Besides being a medical practitioner, he is a practitioner of self-influence, and you rely upon that self-influence.

• Interesting people are self-influenced

The man you may have seen pitch a no-hit, no-run baseball game had to know how to apply self-influence many times during the game. Self-influence was the reserve power that helped him put the ball across the plate so that it couldn't be hit!

The test pilot who takes an untried aircraft on its first flight, goes equipped with experience, skill, nerve and self-influence! If he couldn't depend upon himself, he couldn't fly that plane!

That fine woman who was made an untimely widow, yet who has made the adjustment in life that makes her a wholesome, purposeful person, on her own, knows the power and value of self-influence.

Any person who has inspired you by words or deeds, who has demonstrated a fresh viewpoint or who acts self-confidently, has been motivated by forces he or she marshalled with the power of self-influence.

• Success comes from self-influence

Indeed, self-influenced people do lead the most successful lives. These are the kind of people you are taking your cue from in following the path of self-influence in this book of yours. This indeed is the dynamic factor that master-controls your life. The next step is to learn the skill of self-influence, all the way!

What have you learned about your life? You have become aware of that force that is working ON you, from the outside, and within you, in your mind. This ever-present force is influence, and it master-controls your life. It always has and always will!

• Self-influence for yourself

You now know that you can control this force in your life by cultivating the skill of self-influence. You know that you can make self-influence exert positive control over your life, and you know that you can depend on this kind of control 24 hours a day, every day. Other successful people have done this. The secret of their success has been their determination to influence their own lives, call their own shots, shape their own futures. But there is no secret to learning the skill of self-influence. The determination to learn is the first self-influenced step for you to take, and that is right at hand!

IN SUM

You can learn to control influence.

Influence shapes your life.

Self-controlled influence is the key to success.

Cultivate the skill of self-influence and you will be able to depend on its positive control at all times.

o→ RESULT-GETTING PROJECTS ←o

1. Plot the four areas of influenced action in your everyday life. On another piece of paper, serving as another "working tool" for you, write four "headings" like this:

Physical action: Emotional action: Intellectual action: Spiritual action

Under each heading, list three or four things that you do as part of the everyday pattern of your life. You can probably provide an extended list of "physical actions" but the others may take a bit of consideration. Under "emotional action," are there times when you are happier, more contented and are there times when you are uninspired, even fearful? List them, for these are actions caused by influence. Under "intellectual action," are there times when you "think things through best," read a good book or possibly times when you are mentally fatigued? List them. These, too, are influenced actions. Under "spiritual action," are there times when you truly feel that you are meeting your purpose in life, that you have a feeling of inner peace of mind? Are there times when you feel alone and lonely? Also list these as influenced actions. This project will effectively demonstrate the constancy of influence in your everyday life. Do it as a prelude to a good understanding of this dynamic factor in your own life.

2. Continuing with the paper and pencil, make a "bright star" list of six items that represent accomplishment in your life, where you called the shots that made them happen. You wouldn't be out of line if you put a gold star in front of each item. Please do put these down on paper, because I want you to prove to yourself that the potential for positive self-influence is dynamic in your life!

3. Write down three items that are concerned with the present time in your life.

What self-influenced action are you involved in, or in which you are about to be involved, that positively affects:

    (a) Your home life?
    (b) Your financial status?
    (c) The use of the power of your subconscious mind?

If you are a "good student," and are "doing your home work," you could list all three answers quickly. "a" and "b," for example, could be related to your agreements in Chapter 2. Right? And would you say that "c" is related to your participation, thus far, in your book? I would say it is! Your objective here is prove that this idea of self-influenced action is not a nebulous thing but that, rather, it is related to your life at this moment!

(Again, don't throw this "home-work" away. Better fold it in as a bookmark at this chapter!)

4

Self-Influence Is the Key
to the Pattern
of Your Life

IS YOUR LIFE PERFECT?

No reason for it not to be, even though you might give me a dozen reasons as to why it isn't. I know thousands of persons whose lives you would consider perfect; they all look very much like you, because they are all "humans." Human beings do have the capacity for leading ideal lives, even though you and I know that most of them are on the other side of the fence. For the most part, that "fence" is one they build themselves. Lives less than perfect are as much "home-made" as are those that are right.

• Don't be a fenced-in slave

I knew a husband and wife who apparently hated each other, yet they continued to live together, with a "fence" of their own making between them. I have known hundreds of people who hated their jobs, yet they continued to plod back and forth between job and home each day, like "fenced-in slaves." I have known scores of persons who variously hated the mornings, or the nights, or the week-days, or the week-ends. They even hated the holidays! They had blocked out whole areas of time which they said were "no good" for them. Obviously none of these people had much chance of getting up to the "perfect" standard in life.

But notice that I said I knew these people, as I described them. I knew them as students in the Simmons Institute courses. Through self-influence, they eventually knocked down those fences. The husband and wife really loved each other, and they are now enjoying a blessed life, living together under the influence of expressed love in action. Others have gotten out of the rut and now have inspiring "careers" rather than routine jobs. Still others now use every hour of every day to live a full life, with no blank spots. These people learned, as you are about to learn, that self-influence is the key to a perfect life.

• Your three steps of learning

Yes, the next step is to learn the skill of self-influence for yourself. We are going to tackle this job of "learning" by using those three proven steps of planning, practicing, perfecting. The tempo will be much more accelerated than that which usually marks the process of learning a skill. There aren't going to be any slow, plodding schemes to follow, nor any generalized formulae that fit only one out of a hundred people.

We are concerned with you, and your life, and you can't afford to wait until you are too feeble to enjoy it to have perfection in your life. You and I together are going to make a plan, and, just from the act of making the plan, it is going to have immediate value to you. And you are going to practice.

There will be nothing hypothetical about the practice sessions. Each one will be directly related to your everyday life. "Purely practical" is the slogan for this practice. You are not going to have to wait until you have some kind of "diploma" to be considered competent. Each practice step will bring about a degree of perfection in self-influence.

So, for a short time, we will give all our attention to that plan. You're going to need a piece of paper and a pen or pencil to do your part in this planning. A small piece of paper will do; even a 3 x 5 file card will serve the purpose. You are only going to make a few notes on this paper. After you are through, you are going to leave it, sort of as a bookmark, in the pages of this chapter.

It is most important that you get this paper now and plan on using it. This is no "gimmick" or clever idea. What you put down on this paper will become the basis for the practical practice, with highly desirable results in prospect. You see, this is not to be my plan for you but your plan for yourself. So please put your book down for a moment, and get that paper and pencil!

Thank you! Now both of us are ready to move along.

• The beginning of a good experience

You have never made a plan like *this* one before. Don't make hard work of it. Don't wear a frown. Just take it easy, and everything will go along smooth and easy-like. It is important that you just let this plan form itself, in line with the suggestions I will give you.

It will be much better if you react emotionally rather than ponder at length. This is the beginning of a good experience. Enjoy every moment of it. In fact, our method of making this plan has the attributes of an interesting game.

I am going to put a list of fifteen subjects in front of you now. Imagine that I am handing you a most unusual menu, from which you will make some choices for a most extraordinary "meal." Every one of the items listed represents a basic need or desire in your life. Regardless of how you have lived your life in the past, or the pattern of it in the future, everything you do comes from a fundamental urge that is rooted in one or more of these subjects.

• The choice is yours

Our menu offers the subjects in three groups of five each. Choose one subject from each group. Just one, please! Looking over the whole list, you will probably say: "Why, I really want all of these!" Eventually I'll see that all of them are "served" to you, but just now choose three, as though you were choosing a "balanced meal" from the menu. They will amount to more than a "full meal," for this experience.

Here is where the pencil and paper are necessary. As you choose a subject from each group, you will also answer the question related to it. You will write the title of the subject, and your answer to the question, on the paper. When you have covered the list, you will have written three subject titles and three answers. Simple enough, isn't it? Yes, but this piece of paper is going to become one of your prized possessions!

Just a bit of coaching, before you make your choices. Choose subjects for which you have a *strong feeling* of need or desire. They may be things that you have wanted to have, or to do, for such a long time that, up to this moment, it has seemed as though they would never come true for you. Still, you want them badly. Also be sure that the subjects call for action by you. Be sure that they depend upon your decisions and upon your choice of the kind of action involved. In other words, these should be very personal, strongly wanted choices, which would dynamically affect your life if they could be made to happen.

You are ready, and here is Group One.

1. TIME—a vital factor in your life. What one thing could you do to get more out of the time you devote to a particular period of your everyday life, such as your working hours, your "play" hours, your family-time periods, your reading period, etc.?

2. MONEY—that necessary economic factor in your life. What one thing could you do to increase the value of money that is marked for you, in relation to how you use it? You might be considering budgets, buying habits, talking it over more with your marriage partner, and so forth.

3. ENERGY—that necessary "go-power" in your life. What one thing could you do that would be "above and beyond" your normal program, if you had more energy?

4. HEALTH—the factor that is necessary to maintain life on an even keel. What one habit could you correct, or what new habit could you acquire, that would improve your sense of well-being, of feeling right all the time?

5. THE FUTURE—that distant horizon you always have an eye on. If you could do it, what one thing about your future would you like to see forecast?

All right, you have read the choices in Group One. Now go back and read them over. Make your choice, and answer the question. Now go on to Group Two.

1. LOVE—the source of warmth in your life. In relation to the other person who is close to you, what one thing could you do to strengthen the bond of love between the two of you?

2. CONTENTMENT—that feeling that comes when all's right with the world. What one circumstance or condition in your life could you improve to bring you greater contentment?

3. PEACE OF MIND—the much-sought-after inner feeling

of harmony. What one circumstance or condition in your life would increase in value if you could have peace of mind about it?

4. ADVENTURE—that urge to do something new and different. What one stimulating activity would you be part of if you had the chance to "let yourself go"?

5. BEAUTY or LOOKING YOUR BEST. Obviously, it's "beauty" if you are a woman and "looking your best" if you are a man. In either case, be assured that everybody wants one or the other. What one thing could you do to let your kind of beauty show forth or to meet that standard you want to meet for looking your best?

As you did with the first group, re-read this group. Make your choice and write your answer. Here's Group Three.

1. ACHIEVEMENT—a required action in your life if it is to be a full life. What one thing could you do to be marked with that hallmark of distinction that is given a person who achieves a personal goal?

2. RECOGNITION—without which life is pretty dull. What one activity could you initiate, or what one action could you be part of, that would allow you to use your best talents to good advantage?

3. SELF-EXPRESSION—without which the world would be a most uninteresting place. What one "good idea" do you have that is "ready to pop" and where and how could you let it be known to others?

4. PERSONALITY—that "living display" of the real you. What one thing could you do to best display the best of your personality attributes?

5. HAPPINESS—that ultimate goal for all time. What one thing could you do that would make happiness be so real in your life that you could practically "taste it"?

Once again, re-read the list, make a choice and answer the

question. Now you have done all the "writing" necessary. But hold on to that paper while we establish its important status.

• Stimulating and inspiring prospects

As we consider what you wrote on that paper, we see the beginning of a plan of living that has stimulating and inspiring prospects. Suppose, for example, you have put down energy, peace of mind, and recognition and that you have defined the things you could do to make them realities in your life. There isn't anything better that could happen to you, to make life really worthwhile, than to have three good outcomes from what you do. But let's be sure we read the "fine print" in this proposal. I hope you noticed that I asked you to specify actions that you could do, because "could" means that you can do them. I should caution that you have committed yourself to doing them, because I am now going to lead you into those practice steps—which simply means "doing them."

What you have actually done, in making these choices, is to take the first and basic step in the practice of self-influence. You decided to do some things that are related to urgent needs and desires. You pinned these specific things down as actions you wanted to do, and you have said you can do them. You have overcome that inertia which up to now has made these desired objectives just passive wishes. You have turned on the power, by making a pact with yourself. That power is symbolized by what is on this piece of paper of yours.

• Make a pact with yourself

Why is this paper a source of power, an inanimate thing like this? It is because before you can do anything worthwhile—that is, of your own volition—you must make a pact with yourself by saying: "This I want to do, this I can do." You must influence yourself, first, before you can expect to influence that "what, how and when" of *doing*. And, certainly, you must influence yourself first, with the importance of your plans for action, before you can expect to influence others who will be related to your actions. (Your practice of self-influence in relation to influencing other people is covered in the next chapter.) You are on your way to a bull's-eye score on the subjects you chose.

What happens to the piece of paper now? It stays right here, in your book. Place it as a bookmark at the beginning of this chapter. It will be handy, in this spot, to refer back to as we get into the practice steps. But more than that, this piece of paper, representing the start of your self-influenced program of achievement, tells you that this book certainly is yours. Through the guidance of the succeeding chapters, what you said you WANTED on that list, you will get!

• Remember your agreements

Just a gentle reminder at this point. While this personal plan of yours is "percolating," you are going through with those agreements you made in Chapter 2, aren't you? I am depending on you to do that, because taking those actions will help prepare you for the practice steps in relation to your new plan.

Things have taken a rather active turn, haven't they? You wish you could spend all of your time on such activities. Well, you *will*, eventually. This is only the beginning. But don't pass up a *second* of the enjoyment and stimulation that is related to what you are doing now.

IN SUM

By planning, practicing and perfecting, you can learn the skill of self-influence.

---

o→ RESULT-GETTING PROJECTS ←o

If you really want to build a fire under this self-influenced plan of yours, make a copy of this list of personal choices. Better yet, make a couple of copies. Perhaps you should write them on the back of your business card, or on a piece of colored paper, so that when you see it, it will look like something special. Put one copy of the list in your wallet, or in your purse, so that it stays *with* you during the day. Put another copy in a spot where you are likely to come across it frequently during your working day. For example, place a copy under the glass on top of your desk or on the mirror over your dressing table. Do this and feel the stimulating effect of these reminders of what you have done, reminders of the fact that through self-influence, and *on your own*, you have taken the first step in "calling your own shots."

5

Is Life a Mystery?

HENRY SMITH BUYS STEEL, LOTS OF IT. HE BUYS IT BE-
cause it is his job to keep his firm supplied with steel and
other raw materials from which its products are made. Henry
Smith wants steel, needs steel constantly.

George Brown sells steel. His company's name is well known
in the trade, and it has stayed profitably competitive for many
years. George Brown, who sells steel, calls on Henry Smith,
who needs steel. But Henry doesn't buy, and George doesn't
sell.

Bob Green sells steel, too. His company is reputable, but
no more so than George Brown's company. Bob also calls on
Henry Smith. Henry buys, and Bob sells.

• To him who has shall be given

Why did Bob sell his product, and why did George fail to
do so? Both men were offering good steel to a man who

needed steel. Why did Henry Smith buy from one and not the other?

The answer is a mystery to George, but it is no mystery to Bob. And the answer has nothing to do with the tangible product in question. The same question could be asked about two people applying for a job with an employer who needs help badly. The two applicants could be equally well qualified for the position, yet one is readily chosen over the other, the mystery of "why" hangs over the head of the rejected applicant.

• **People make life a mystery**

No, the mystery of "why" isn't related to the product offered for sale or to the technical qualifications of the applicants. The mystery is related to people, and the answer is related to people. Life is a mystery only if people make it so. I'll prove that to you.

Up to this point, I have been asking you to take quite a bit on faith. I have been guiding you into experiences which have most unusual slants to them. And I have been telling you that there will be certain outcomes if you do certain things. The outcomes I have been predicting are uncommon in the lives of most people, so why should I have such confidence in forecasting them in your life?

It could seem as though I am asking you just to have faith in me until I can cause something dramatic to happen to you. But this isn't so. Most certainly I want you to have faith in me, as a person. I should want that to be if I were your neighbor and your friend, or your working associate, or if we were just having a cup of coffee together. I consider it a privilege to warrant your faith. In our present relationship, I am simply the interpreter of some facts in this, your book. I feel that I warrant your faith in my role as spokesman and, I hope, "teacher" of a good way of life, because this book is the culmination of more than a quarter century of the same relationship with many thousands of people.

• Focus your faith on your whole life

But none of this is intended to be the focal point of your faith. I want you to focus your faith on life itself, in a way of living that can help mankind meet its best destiny and, above all, in yourself. For these reasons, you were guided into establishing evidence of the value of your own importance to yourself. For these reasons, you were asked in the last chapter to make that initial "plan," based upon those fundamental urges of yours. And for these reasons you should know that there is no mystery to life. The true meaning of life is manifest all about you, and it takes only a self-influenced open mind to have it revealed to you.

Life has been labeled a "mystery" because two questions have been left unanswered in the lives of too many people. Two big questions that live like a parasite in people's lives are: "What should I do, and what will the outcome be if I do make a choice?" Another apparent enigma is: "How can I have *more* positive, and *fewer* negative, conditions in my life?"

Permitting influences to combine willy-nilly to have unpredictable effects in their lives causes many persons to assume that they are not supposed to be able to "call the shots" very often and that they just have to expect negative effects to outnumber positive ones. This leads to a resigned, submissive attitude—the attitude of a person with little faith in himself or in life. It leads to private thoughts in which a person says to himself: "I wish I knew how to be more successful and happier. I wish I could get rid of these fears and anxieties." He looks enviously at the lives of persons who go through life with "all the flags flying," and he believes that they either "got all the breaks" or that they are blessed geniuses.

You know people like that, with resigned, submissive attitudes. Perhaps there have even been times when you have felt that way yourself. In any case, just where do thoughts and attitudes like that originate? They are born, and they continue to live, within the person himself! If we were looking for a dramatic example, none would be more striking than this demonstration of tragic self-influence. Such people have influenced themselves to let those two questions remain questions in their lives. They are making life a mystery!

• Self-influence builds up faith

Of course you know the antidote for all this. It is self-influence, with a completely positive slant to it, and subsequent action that will bring answers to those two questions. Left unanswered, those two questions prompt many to call life a mystery. It is having faith in life, in your own pattern of living and in yourself that will give you the answers.

True faith is based upon trust, and trust is based upon understanding. It is hard to trust another person, or an environmental condition, or a relationship, you do not understand. Even more to the point is that a person who doesn't understand himself really can't trust himself, because he can't predict his reactions.

On the other hand, your own experience has proved that if you understand another person, you can even disagree with him and still trust him. You have found that if you try to understand our social customs and laws, you are more inclined to have faith in them than if you delved into only one side. Such understanding comes from open-mindedness, the great attribute of a positively self-influenced person.

• To understand yourself—understand others

The best way to induce faith in yourself, and in life, is to have a good understanding of all people. Understanding people—the children of the Creator and as your "brothers" in the life-span alloted you—removes any "mystery" about life, simply because people are life! In this sense, all people are created "equal." A "likeness" in the pattern of life of all people is to be expected. This "likeness" is the basis of the society of mankind, and there are many reasons to be thankful for it and to have faith in it. All people have the same fundamental, human urges. Prompting everyone's actions are the urges for self-preservation, for self-expression, for recognition, for love and affection, for adventure. Thus, when you see a person acting in a certain way—which you do not understand and which might lead you to mistrust him—you can become an astute observer of human behavior by doing just one thing. Try to relate his actions to one of those basic urges and thus learn why he is acting this way. You will find that he is trying to satisfy one of the same kind of urges you have. You might not want to copy his actions, but now you understand him.

Nine times out of ten, this kind of understanding will prove that there is no reason at all to mistrust him. His methods may not appeal to you, but his motive is good. You find that you can get along fine together, he in his way and you in yours. You find that you can even be friends!

• There are people with wrong motives

However, we cannot close our eyes to that possible one time out of a hundred when your search for understanding reveals a person whose motives are wrong. Sometimes people like this flash across the world like a fireball, apparently hell-bent on knocking everybody and everything down in their perverted urge for recognition and self-expression. Sometimes such people become petty irritants, apparently wanting to run contrary to the accepted code of society.

I am not suggesting that you close your eyes to the fact that such people do exist. But I do call your attention to the fact that such behavior among people is over-emphasized in the reporting and publishing of what is happening every day in this world of ours. Sensational news seems to be the only news when we evaluate what we read about everyday. If you read and hear, for example, only what is reported as the story of the "passing scene," you would get the feeling that things were always at a negative crisis stage in our national government. Yet, behind the scenes, thousands of people are doing superb jobs every day in rendering service as governmental representatives. This is so regardless of which party is in power at the moment!

You only have to read one of the thousands of books about people who have accomplished good things, who have inspirational messages to tell, or who are telling about how to do the good things, to know that the majority of people do have the right motives. You have only to consider all of the people you know, and to apply the principle of "understanding" to them, to learn that they all have good motives. If you find even one whose motives are questionable, you will find that he is mentally, physically or morally ill. That, too, you can understand, and possibly you can even help him.

- **Faith in others brings faith in life**

What is the significance of these observations of a true understanding of people? It means that most of the time you can have faith in people. It means that you can justify this faith with a self-influenced attitude of open-mindedness. It means that most people are like you, in that they want to live good lives. For these reasons, you can have faith in life. It means that in a test of the pattern of life in our world today, you will find that the motives of the greatest majority are good. I agree that you will find that not enough individuals are motivated strongly enough to live as they want to live. But that is no reason not to trust them or not to have faith in their relationships to your life. You have great reason to be thankful that you are like most people in many respects, since this means that you can place your faith in this "union" of people who believe in the "Fatherhood of God and the brotherhood of man." Help this "union" be strong by influencing yourself to have faith in it!

• Distinctiveness is your birthright

Yes, you are an "equal" as far as most people are concerned. But along with that equality that is inherent in your birthright, you were created as a *distinctive* person; you were endowed with a distinctive purpose in life. It was part of the Creator's plan that you be endowed with this distinctiveness. Whatever your academic interpretation of the Supreme Being is, I know that it includes faith in His word to His children. Viewed objectively, His word is to live according to His laws and to live a purposeful life, according to your own standards. This last part of His word is what makes you distinctive. It means that as you have faith in Him, you will also have faith in yourself and have faith in your standards of living a good life.

• Does God help those who help themselves?

Consider what has been said here. Consider it carefully, because it removes all the "mystery" from life. We have said that you are like all other people in many respects and that you could prove this by understanding others. But we have also said that you are unlike others in many respects. This is an intentional distinctiveness that is your birthright. This distinctiveness tells you that you can and should live your own life, with faith in yourself. Why does all of this cancel out any mystery of life? Simply because it makes a glaring truth out of that popular adage, "God helps those who help themselves."

Look around you and see what is happening to others. With an open-minded observation, you see that people who are progressively helping themselves are also getting "help" from many other sources. They are not getting "lucky breaks." They aren't geniuses. They are simply controlling the influences that surround them. With an open mind, with an alert mind, they deliberately seek answers to those two big questions in life. They expect to find the answers, because they have influenced themselves to have faith in life. They find the answers, because they have faith in themselves. Under that kind of plan of living, there is no "mystery" to life!

• Join the club

You can join this "no mystery to life" club. In fact, you have already paid your initiation fee if you have completed those "agreements" you made with yourself in Chapter 2.

Why have these actions removed the mystery from life? Consider the results with an open mind and you will see why. As the result of those agreements, you demonstrated a belief of yours by taking part in a progressive activity. And you proved that you trusted another person by serving him. What else is there to life except to have beliefs, to act progressively and to get along with others? An everyday diet of that kind of living is almost ideal, isn't it? And you have just had an **experience with that kind of living. That experience was the** result of the influence you had over your own actions. Is there any reason why you cannot repeat and repeat this pattern? No reason at all! No reason, that is, as long as you keep an open mind and understand what you are doing. There just can't be any mystery to a life like that!

But it all depends upon that factor of faith. It depends upon your having faith in yourself!

IN SUM

Faith in yourself, in others and in life stems from understanding.

This faith dispels the "mystery" of life.

Faith enables you to see that you can help yourself.

---

o→ RESULT-GETTING PROJECTS ←o

Expand your relationship with this concept of faith by expanding your experience with it. When you were deciding upon the actions that are related to those original three agreements you made in Chapter 2, there were several choices you could have made for each, weren't there? Those that you did choose probably were the most appropriate, according to the terms of that project. Reconsider those possible choices that were not included in that project. Consider those actions which might require a bit more "push" to get them going. There are some things related to a belief, or progressive action, or service, that you should have done long ago. Perhaps some of these may have assumed the role of an "obligation" or "duty," by now, and you might be inclined to feel a bit embarrassed over your avoidance of them. Now, make up another set of three agreements where action requires you to "take a deep breath and plunge in." Within the next 24 hours, act according to these agreements.

A safe prediction is that the meaning of faith will appear like a neon-lighted sign in your life, both because of the effect of this action within you and the effect from the response of others who are affected by your actions. You will prove that faith in yourself takes care of the "hard" things as well as the "easy" ones.

6

Is There a Superior Race
in the Making?

SOMETHING IS HAPPENING IN THE WORLD TODAY THAT IS more powerful than atomic power, or hydrogen bombs, or anything else controlled by man that you can possibly conceive of!

This "something" is a power that is building up within certain people. It is putting almost unlimited power in their muscles, in their minds, in their hearts and, yes, in their very souls!

This power is building up in the lives of more and more people, because more and more people are learning to create this power within themselves. This power is making them superior people, masters of themselves and, therefore, potentially masters of the world.

• The person you see in the mirror

This superior power may be present in the next person you meet. Conceivably it is present in the life of any truly successful person you know. But more important, it can be created in the person you see when you look in the mirror!

A moment ago I spoke of your membership in the "no mystery to life" club. I qualified for membership some time ago, and I want to welcome you to the fraternity! You and I are in the best of company, in this brotherhood. The members don't wear badges or special regalia. You will recognize a "brother" or "sister" by their air of self-confidence, by their relationship to progressive circumstances and by their attitude of "all's right with the world." And they will recognize you as a fellow-member as you display the same "signs" of faith in yourself and the world. "Meetings" are held whenever two or more "members" happen to get together. Try to be part of such a "meeting" yourself, two or three times a day. There is nothing better than to renew your faith in the principles of the club!

• Making men masters of themselves

Now that you have joined this "club," you can qualify for another, rather exclusive association of people. Most of the members of our "club" belong to this one, too. This is the "better world through better people" club. Its slogan is "Make men masters of themselves."

Sound fantastic, over-idealistic or even slightly "crack-pot"? It could very well seem so to people who refuse to look at its objectives with an open mind, without an effort to understand. Frankly, membership in this group is limited to persons who practice self-influence to the highest degree. There is no *intent* that membership be on an "exclusive" basis. Apparently most people don't want to join, so the group is a minority group. Whether it grows to a majority, or fades from the face of the earth, depends upon people like you and me.

• **The power that is building up**

Should you support this movement? I'll leave that to your judgment. Here are the facts about it. This movement goes a step beyond the "no mystery to life" concept. It proposes that not only is there "no mystery" but that there are potentials for a "superior race" in the world. Its supporters believe that this can become a possibility when more and more people understand and practice positive self-influence. They have a practical set of plans, and they are working the plans. They invite you to join with them if you believe that you are a candidate for this "superior race."

• **Progressiveness is in the air**

There are many obvious factors that support this viewpoint. This movement takes its cues from four different conditions that exist among people today. First is the display of progressiveness coming from programs and leadership in the fields of religion, education, and social practice. The church, per se, has become more than ever an integrated factor in the lives of more and more people. The widest choice of educational opportunities is freely offered to more people. In the social order, many more practical, all-inclusive programs are in force, underwriting the security and welfare of more people. Your own inventory of what you see happening in these fields proves this display of mass progressiveness. This "superior race" movement believes that all of this is a demonstration of mass influence that helps point the way toward its goal.

Then second, there is the display of technological progress that is so obvious today. We have almost come to take for granted that the "impossible" will become a "certainty" in the technical fields. "You name it and it can be done," seems to be the motto here. We used to say about a person who was extravagant in his ideas: "He wants the moon, with a little red fence around it!" Today, a person wouldn't be asking for "too much," if he said he wanted the moon! Somebody is liable to organize a "rocket party" and go up and get it for him! Our "better world" movement points to this "limitless" technological program as another demonstration of mass influence that supports their objectives.

• Many people need help

Third, the movement points to a fundamental psychological factor that exists in people's lives. This is based upon the observation that people seem to respond more "naturally" to negative influences than to positive ones. Apparently people do not have to "learn" to respond to influences that induce fear, anxiety, doubt or guilt feelings. Of course there is a protective instinct prompting some of these reactions, but we do seem to respond more readily to such influences than to influences stemming from happiness, good-will or confidence. Apparently we have to "learn" from experience to respond more readily to positive influences. This "better world" movement believes that this psychological factor *causes* a need that each individual has. It is, therefore, a need that the world has and it sees the possibility of mass influence, for the good of all.

Finally, the movement points to the mass negative influences that exist in the world, at any one moment, and it reminds us of the great lessons that can be learned from those conditions. The dictator philosophy of leadership is an example. World-wide, we see this manifest itself in some national governments. Closer to home, we see it in the action of a few individuals, perhaps in our vocational relationship, in our community and, sometimes, even in the home. In back of this kind of leadership is pressure influence, i.e., influence by fear, by duress, by subjugation. Invariably the success of such leadership is dependent upon force. The people interested in our movement ask you to consider why this pressure and force is necessary. You will reach the same conclusion that they have, that force is necessary because people are being influenced to act *against their wills*. In some form or other, negative "brain washing" is necessary to the perpetuation of dictatorships. The great lesson to be learned from this is that the only way to effectively resist "slave" leadership is to help more and more people learn the skill of self-influence. That would seem like a herculean task, yet it is part of the program of this movement.

• Participation pays off

Those are the facts. Now here is the program of this movement. The goal is to have more and more people participate in life as strong, important individuals. The goal is to make it unpopular to be just a spectator in life and to let whatever happens just happen! The method agreed upon is based upon more and more people having the same kind of an experience with self-influence that you are having right now, as participants, and not as spectators.

The people associated with these objectives are committed to putting them into action by giving of themselves, by sharing and by being living examples of positive self-influence.

There you have it, the story of this "better world through better people" club. Will you support it? Do you believe that there is such a movement? Would you join such a movement?

There is no movement as such, with a "constitution and by-laws." But there are many people who believe in its principles and who believe that such a program would bring about a superior race. They do act as though they were committed to those principles. They feel this way and act this way because, although no such superior race will probably exist in their lifetimes, they want to qualify for that status, anyway. They have learned that such qualification supports their own patterns of life, as formed by self-influenced principles.

• An invitation to progress

My associates in the Simmons Institute "belong" to this movement. Students of our Home Study Course "belong" to it. Every person that you know of who has made a worthwhile contribution to the world, to any degree, and who at the same time has acted to support his own distinctiveness, "belongs" to the movement.

Here is why we belong. I recommend that you consider them as reasons for your belonging, too. First, we believe in the principle involved. But beyond that, the reasons are purely personal, because they support our personal programs of self-influence. Since there are those mass programs in the fields of religion, education and social practice that have a progressive influence, the best way that we can take advantage of them personally is as supporting participants. Since the technological field is pointing the way to superior mass accomplishment, the best way we can take advantage of this personally is to support and use the good results.

Considering that psychological factor that tends to put negative influences above positive ones, we each know how to combat this with self-influence, just as you are learning to do. But it is to the personal advantage of each of us to have more people practicing the same skill because, as the mass average of positive influence goes up, we strengthen our own positions. Therefore, it is to our advantage to serve others by helping them understand self-influence and by showing them how. Thus, we are contributing to the creation of such a desirable mass influence and improving our own lives at the same time.

• Service to others is good business

Service to others is also the basis of our interest in the negative influences that exist in the world. These man-made influences seem to have such strength, to be so aggressive, to have organized domination. We believe that positively influenced people can display great strength, can be equally aggressive and can eventually dominate world conditions. The fact that this is a staggering goal doesn't deter us in the least from doing what we can now, in the belief that a better tomorrow is possible. We believe that by being good examples of self-influence, we are giving courage to others who are struggling to overcome "slave" leadership. We know that a better world is dependent upon masses of individually "better people." So we support the idea because it is our world, too.

There is a familiar ring to those reasons why we "belong," isn't there? There *is*, because they are absolutely parallel to those three "agreements" (Chapter 2) that you are involved in with yourself. Yes, this "better world movement" is also based upon *belief* that is demonstrated, upon relationship to progressive action and upon service to others. Participation in this movement will take you above and beyond the status of self-influence that can result if you simply try to go it alone. This is so because there is an uncontestable law related to such participation. This law says that every time you give to others in a positive fashion, you receive much more in return.

• Become a member

Two simple actions will start your participation in this movement. One is to get others interested in a program of self-influence. Help them "see the light" by becoming a missionary for the movement. Get others to read this book, too, so that you will have fellow workers close to you. The other way is to join organizations and groups that are working in the field of mass positive influence.

Is such a movement a realistic basis for a "superior race"? It most certainly is, because a "master race" must be composed of individually superior people. Superior people are those who are positively self-influenced. A "union" of such people, even though they may be a minority group today, could very well be called today's superior race. Aggressive minority groups have, in the past, brought about much of human progress. The prospect of a "better world through better people" is a possibility, provided more people become masters of themselves, even as you and we are.

It takes only a self-influenced decision on your part to make you a candidate for this "superior race." Will you serve others as you serve yourself, in the support of positive influences?

I believe that the contents of the next chapter will help you make this decision.

IN SUM

A "better" world is dependent on the development of "better" people.

"Better" people are those who have understanding and practice self-influence.

● ● ●

SUMMARY OF PART ONE
YOUR PLAN

• You have been introduced to self-influence, to the power of the subconscious.

• You have taken several preliminary steps to assure yourself of its existence.

• You have decided what kind of person you want to be.

• This you have done with the knowledge that you are important and have a purpose in life.

• You have planned.

• Now you are ready for a more penetrating investigation of the phenomenon of self-influence.

• You are also ready for the next step—practice.

● ● ●

PART TWO

YOUR PRACTICE

7

The Latest Models
in Human Beings

ONE OF THE SOCIAL PRACTICES ACCEPTED IN CERTAIN other parts of the world but frowned on by our Western civilization is the idea of a harem. Other than the moral side of it, the idea just doesn't add up in our way of thinking.

But have you ever wondered just how one of those harem princes goes about picking his wives? Does he look for variety, or likeness? Does he have some kind of standards that he goes by? Does he pick the latest wife like most of us buy cars, by choosing the latest, smartest model that catches our eye?

I don't suppose that you or I will ever know the answers, and I'm sure we won't lose any sleep over those questions. But this idea of picking and choosing different "models" of people is not limited to princes who are looking for fifth or sixth wives. You picked a certain "model" for your marriage partner, and you have picked certain other "models" for your friends.

• What model are you?

But how about yourself? Have you picked a new "model" of yourself, for yourself, recently? Or haven't you thought of that possibility. Perhaps you haven't considered it possible.

Well, it's time now to consider whether the current "model" of you is up-to-date or whether you should consider a trade-in.

We are about to leave the planning stage in your experience with self-influence. We have already stepped over the line a bit into the practice stage, practice that has been in the nature of preparation for the full-scale practice that is coming. But good planning involves one more step, which is exactly where you are now, as far as your life is concerned at this moment. It is most important to take a "personal inventory," because this is the only way you will know what to do, specifically, in the practice steps. You must know what specific changes you want to make in your habits and attitudes and what specific actions to take to make those changes.

• Being objective pays dividends

I want this to be a revealing, and a stimulating, experience for you. So I ask you to prepare yourself through the practice of a bit of self-influence. Do you know what "objectivity" means and what it means to be "objective"? These are commonly used words, of course, but they also have common interpretations that are superficial. I want you to practice objectivity, but I want you to know—really know—its value and to be truly objective. If you are in doubt, see what your dictionary says they mean. Briefly, objectivity means to concentrate on the reality of something that has external shape, form, or action, without "coloring" that something with wishful thinking. To be objective means to see the basic truth.

So, in the privacy that exists between just you and your book, you are going to take a realistic look at yourself and at your life, which has shape, form and action related to it. Will you make the agreement with yourself, therefore, to be objective?

• Choose your model

I am going to line up several kinds of people, through word pictures. These represent the latest models in human beings, as they exist in today's world. Out of this "line up," you will choose the models about which you will say: "That one is just like me" or "That one is like I want to be." You will find that the choices you make will add strength to your plan. Incidentally, as each model appears, put a "skirt" or "trousers" on it, to match the variety of "model" you are.

• Many people are like this model

Here is model Number 1. This is a person who lives in an emotional whirlpool. He sees the world as a dark, unfriendly place where circumstances and conditions are always plotting against him. He is suspicious of the motives of others, yet he won't ever let himself be exposed to mutual understanding. He has great fear of doing the wrong thing at the wrong time. He is apprehensive of the future, almost on a day-by-day basis. He creates a false security by withdrawing from any pattern of participation that he is not forced into. Outside influences have built up stresses and tensions in his life that make it a private "hell on earth." He is probably the least self-influenced of any of the models.

• Here's a model you see often

Model Number 2. Life is filled with question marks for this
one. He is the "worry-wart" variety who seems to enjoy not
finding answers to the questions in his life. He is inclined to
say about a specific "answer" that has been pointed out: "Yes,
that's possible, but I just don't believe it!" He isn't the passive
type, by any means. He does get some things done in life, but
always the hard way because he sees life as one big problem.
Self-influence with him is overshadowed by a maze of half-
truth influences from the outside.

• This one matches people you know

Model Number 3. This model's life is full of good intentions.
In fact, he is so full of them, it could be said that they represent his major activity in life. He sees most of the desirable
things that society has to offer and he thinks they are just fine.
He wouldn't mind having most of them related to his life. To
that extent, at least, he has a concept of self-influence. But he
"talks to himself" too much about these good things, and he
does too little about action. This is the person who goes
through life wishfully and hopefully. His actions are those of
a person who is stumbling along.

• This model looks better than it acts

Model Number 4. Here is a person who is well equipped
in many ways to live a purposeful, rewarding life. His education has been adequate. He has tried his hand at enough different activities to really know where his best abilities lie. He
knows "black from white" and has the capacity for good understanding. Yet he always seems to be just starting up the

ladder to success. Time never seems to work in his favor. This is the person who fails to go all the way with his knowledge of self-influence. He uses it only periodically or until some irritating outside influence throws him off the track. He isn't like the wishful thinker. This person knows what to do, but he fails to capitalize on that knowledge.

● **You see this model stalled quite often**

Model Number 5. This is the person who talks himself into being a spectator in life, rather than a participant. He is a prime example of the effects of negative self-influence. He feels that he could do a lot of progressive things if there weren't so many other people who were able to do them so much better than he can. He has convinced himself that he can't stand up to competition. He has built up a fear of competition. He fails to see that competition improves his chances for success, because it establishes realistic goals to work for. So he withdraws to the more "comfortable" position of being just a spectator.

● **Here's the most wanted model**

Model Number 6. This is the person who is going along steadily and surely on a program of his own making. He has admirably fitted his program into that of the world about him, and at times he even induces some of the world's program to fit his! His program of living is basically self-influenced, yet he also makes sure that he aligns himself with the best outside influences. Knowing that other people and environmental conditions can be influenced, he does influence them at times when the results will be advantageous to all concerned. He is a member of the "no mystery to life" club, and he is an active participant in the "better world through better people" movement. He would certainly be among those present, if the members of that "superior race" were called together.

There you have six models of human beings. Consider any person you know, and you can say that he or she is like one of those models. Now, what about yourself? Having been objective about it, I know that you have seen images of yourself as these models were paraded before you.

• You can be the model you choose

However, I intended this to be a realistic experiment, just as I intended you to have an objective relationship to it. So I don't think that any one model fits your circumstances. I am sure that you found that parts of more than one model better described your pattern of life up to this point. And that is as it should be, considering your distinctiveness, as well as your "alikeness," to others. But whatever combination does describe you, objectively, it is a most valuable bit of knowledge to have, as I will prove to you in a moment. Just now, I want to acknowledge that I know you have made another choice from those models. I know that you chose Number 6 as the ideal model for yourself. It is ideal for you, and I ask you to accept that model as your objective.

Having acquired an objective picture of yourself, there is nothing to be ashamed of in knowing the "why and wherefore" of the truth about yourself. You aren't seeing anything that you really haven't known before, except that now you are defining the things that you want to change in your life. This, in itself, has been a commendable experience in self-influence. Few people seem to have the fortitude to face up to such truths; YOU have, and you are a better person for it.

• Trade in that old model

Here is the practical side of this self-influence. As we move more and more into the practice steps, you can relate every one of them directly to one of those specific circumstances you want to change in your life. We will be able to acquire a replacement model, one that will be exactly like that model Number 6. What is more, as you grow from practice to perfection in self-influence, you will be able to keep that model up-to-date at all times!

IN SUM

Be objective.

This is to say, see the basic truth in evaluating yourself.

Then, and only then, will you know what changes you will want to make in your habits and attitudes.

Then, and only then, will you know what actions you can and must take to make those changes.

○→ RESULT-GETTING PROJECT ←○

Spend some time analyzing Model No. 6, the one that we agree is ideal for you. Point by point, consider what makes this model "ideal."

Then go back over those other five models and consider
again what parts of them combine to make a simulated
model of you, today. As you do this, those elements that
seem to fit you now all line up as something lacking in
your life. The greatest lack appears to be the right action
at the right time.

All right, now consider those lacking elements that fit
you and compare them with your analysis of Model No. 6.
You will find that, in Model 6, there is a counterpart of
positive action for everyone of those elements representing a lack in your life! If, for example, the model is faced
with a difficult problem, he acts quickly, and with determination, to solve that problem. He does not procrasti-
nate. Are you as positive?

Do this analysis, and this comparison, and you will have
revealed to you the realness of that Model 6, when you
imagine an ideal life for yourself. Your objective is thus
established to make this model real, in the form of yourself!

8

The Subconscious Mind Is the Key to Self-Influence

SUPPOSE SOMEONE CAME UP TO YOU AND SAID: "HERE, I'm putting $1,000,000 at your disposal. Get going on that wonderful idea you've been dreaming about. I'll be your silent partner, but you call all the shots!"

What would you do? Would you take the money? Sure you would! You might think that the fellow was crazy, but certainly you wouldn't argue with such a benefactor.

Well, I know that neither you nor anyone else is going to hold his breath until such a miracle comes his way. But you can make another kind of miracle happen, for yourself, because you do have a silent partner worth one million dollars!

• A million dollar value

Perhaps this sounds like we are kicking around a million dollars like a government appropriations committee. But that's

69

spending money. The million I'm referring to is buying money. If you could have the kind of a life you want, wouldn't it be worth a million? Well, that's exactly what you can "buy" with the help of this silent partner of yours, a "million dollar value" for yourself. Just keep that thought in mind, and let's you and I take time out to talk about it.

We've been going along a pretty steady clip on this "sight-seeing tour" of life, and I'd like you to take a bit of a breather while we just chat for a few moments. We're about to take off in a new direction and see some most unusual "sights." Before we do, I want you to put a completely intimate, personal slant on what has happened so far.

I am pretty sure that by now you have gotten a lot of things sorted out, about yourself, about other people and about why things are as they are with humans. But I am also sure that about now you feel as though you could use some help. You may feel that I have dangled a wonderful "promise" just out of your reach and that if you grab for it, it is likely to elude you.

• STOP! LOOK! LISTEN!

DON'T grab for it! You will get a handful of "nothing" if you try. There is a "promise" right in front of you. The whole point in stopping a moment here is to show you how to turn that "promise" into a certainty, just by thinking about it the right way!

We have been talking a lot about influence. Perhaps you know more about "controlling" that influence than you are aware of. Let's see how good you are at creating an atmosphere that will help you do a bit of concentrated thinking. Here is one way I am certain you can do it.

From your collection of good memories, recall some pleasant, colorful place that has left a pleasant taste in your memory. It could be indoors or outdoors, some place you have visited often, or an enchanted site you visited a long time ago. But what you are recalling is an Elysian spot that has just the right atmosphere for you, sort of a personal paradise.

• Visit your private world

Yours might be like a favorite spot of mine. It's on top of a little hill on a California ranch that my family and I own. I can go up there and see for miles around. I can see and feel the work of nature and of man all around me, and yet be satisfied with just my own company. It's a wonderful spot for refreshing thinking. By mentally recalling this spot, I am there right now!

Whatever your favorite "retreat" spot is, transport yourself there now, in your imagination, except, that this time, imagine that I am with you. I know that this would be an ideal situation in which we could pause and think about that promise for a few moments. Let us imagine that I have taken the book into my hands now, and that you are going to sit back while I read to you and that you listen with attentive willingness. Do this, and you have mentally created an atmosphere that is "right" for this moment. You have induced a desirable influence that will pay dividends in a most realistic manner. With the aid of this influence, let's briefly reconsider all that has been said so far in your book. Then let me show you clearly what is just ahead.

• You know yourself better

We have defined your importance in the scheme of human life, and you have had some specific experiences which prove it. You have become aware of the all-powerful factor of influence, and you are much more aware of its effects than you ever have been before. I am sure that you have acquired a respect for influence, knowing as you do now how completely it affects your life. You now know much more about yourself, and about others. You know that influence has created all kinds of people, ranging from the "unfortunate," to the apparently "blessed" kind. I am sure that by now you have "classified" yourself as being similar to one of the "kinds" of people we have discussed and that you have a pretty clear picture of how past influences established you in that class.

But what is much more important, you now have a new picture of the kind of person you want to be. I concur with this "new look" idea. This is the way you should be. It is the way you will be, and that is a promise I assure you will be kept!

• Face this question boldly

However, superimposed over this sketch of this new you could be a big question mark, saying: "Is it possible?" If this question mark is there, it does not mean that any of your thoughts should be censured. It simply means that you have become intelligently aware of what you need to make that picture clear and strong.

That question mark is there because you have become acutely aware of the need for more and more self-influence, in the future. We can remove the question mark by learning how to boost up self-influence; that help is just around the corner for you. But it must be a specific approach, both as to the structure of that question mark and as to your conduct in using that help. So, what about that question mark?

You will find an interpretation of your question mark in the explanation that follows. It is related to a similar enigma in the lives of others, as well as in your life.

There seems to be an undue amount of pressure on your life from outside influences. There seems to be an inevitable pattern to the influences which surround you. So many of them seem to be controlled by circumstances that would bear down on you like ponderous steam rollers, if you tried to resist them. These could be things like your financial status and the apparent "outside" influences affecting it. Or they could be like any plans you have for the future and the apparently unpredictable, and possibly disturbing, influences that might affect them.

• The effects of wrong influence

Some of the apparent inevitableness of this outside influence is reflected in everyday experiences. Too many times you have said: "It's right on the tip of my tongue, but . . ." Self-influence was here overpowered by outside influence that prevented you from expressing yourself adequately. Often you have foregone a desirable activity with the resigned expression of, "The spirit is willing, but the flesh is weak." You wanted to do something, but the outside influence of apparently unwanted fatigue made you unwillingly withdraw. Many times you have said to yourself: "If I had only done this, instead of that, the outcome would have been much better." In such cases, outside influences negatively dominated your capacity for good judgment. And then there were the times you berated yourself with: "If I had only seen what was coming, I'd have acted differently." Actually, in such cases, you were in a "fog" of outside influences that caused you to make fuzzy decisions. And, of course, there have been those recurring thoughts that come after discussions you have been part of. In retrospect, you can think of all kinds of wonderful things you *could* have said. Here, outside influences had infiltrated into your conscious mind, blocking out the use of your fine resources for contributing "good ideas" at the right time.

Yet, in the face of all of this, you now know what your

choices of action would be *in the future,* if you could influence yourself to act according to those choices. The question
is "how" to influence yourself, isn't it?

• Good things aren't cheap

You see that the answer is related to personal actions that
have high "price tags" on them, and you have some doubt as
to whether your personal resources are great enough for you
to afford these good things. All good things have high "price
tags" on them, but, through the power of self-influence, there
isn't a single one that you can't afford!

Among these high "priced" personal actions, you now see
the need for the self-influence of more good judgment, a better score on decisions, good timing, the display of good ideas,
the fire of enthusiasm and a maintained sense of well-being.

Does not all of this about sum up the structure of that question mark about you and self-influence? Good! This sets a pattern of action, with the answers helping you establish yourself as the kind of a person you should be. However, it could
appear as though you would have to be some kind of a super-
being to switch the pattern of influence in your life. Tackling
it all alone could add a discouraging note to the whole idea.
But you do not have to go it alone! You have a "partner" more
than willing to give you a helping hand. In fact, if you don't
bring this "partner" into the game with you, you won't even
get to first base in perfecting the pattern of self-influence in
your life.

• A perfect partnership

You met this "partner" earlier in your book. You have already
had enough good experience with it to have faith in it. This
partner of yours is, of course, your subconscious mind, and its

power is at your command to give you control of influence in your life. What your subconscious partner can and will do for you is this: It will change the predominate pattern of influence in your life from outside to inside, from uncontrolled outside influence pressure to controlled, self-influenced power inside of you. It will put the "balance of power" in your hands!

Let's consider what kind of a partner your subconscious is. A partner, of course, should support you, should share experiences with you, should participate with you in everything you do and should be on your side. That's the kind of a partner your subconscious is. It has always been willing to be such. What's more, there isn't anything new about this. The subconscious has always been the key to self-influence, for all time and for all people.

• Don't go it alone

Every "self-made" person—every person of importance—has formed a working alliance with this partner. No one ever went it alone in a progressive, successful life. No one ever could, because the subconscious is the key to controlling the influence in everyone's life! What has happened, however, is that science has recently been able to define the subconscious and to give shape and form to its effects. Its power, and how to use it, is no longer a secret. The technique of using it has been developed by science in the hope that a better world would emerge from the effects of its power in the lives of individuals. The opportunity is freely given to you here to become a practitioner of the skill of subconscious self-influence.

• You can be a creator and a controller

Subconscious self-influence means the creation and control of influences by yourself, for yourself. Your subconscious is a marvelous human machine. It might be likened to one of those "mechanical brains," those robot machines that seem to be able to come up with almost any kind of an answer. But your subconscious is capable of doing much more, because it is related to your spirit, to your soul. It is the core of a potential power which can make you be what you should be, act as you want to act and accomplish what you want to accomplish in life. Your subconscious can create positive influences and it can control your actions according to those influences. Thus, all elements of that "question mark" that is before you can be erased and that picture of the new you can be painted in permanent colors.

This is a good point to terminate our little chat and for me to hand the book back to you. It has been good to have these few moments to think things through, hasn't it? You know just where you stand now, and with the stimulating prospect of using subconscious self-influence, let's move on toward the next high point, to the point where you are using it deliberately.

• Subconscious self-influence is the key

Step by step I am going to open up this treasure chest of the power of your subconscious. Each step of the way, your control over self-influence will increase. If there ever was any truth to the statement that "knowledge is power," it is doubly true about what is ahead for you.

Let's move along then. But remember, you are not alone! That partner of yours is going right along with you!

Incidentally, did you notice what happened to the atmosphere around you, when I suggested that we "move along"? It "broke the spell" of being in that imagined quiet spot, just thinking. The new atmosphere is one in which you anticipate doing something. Both were subconsciously created, by letting your subconscious be your working partner, to cause to happen what you wanted to happen. Remember this is an "ABC" step in relation to what is coming.

IN SUM

You have a powerful partner—your subconscious mind.

This partner will help you in developing and perfecting self-influence.

It will enable you to control your life.

---

o→   RESULT-GETTING PROJECTS   ←o

In this project, you will do something that will be a first experience, possibly, for you. But it will be something that you are going to do time and time again in the future and find stimulating and refreshing.

Now, instead of *imagining* yourself on a "retreat," actually set one up for yourself. It will take a bit of planning and stage setting. There is a time in the day when you can be by yourself, when you can be relaxed and undisturbed. Even fifteen minutes in the breakfast nook, after the rest of the household is in bed, will serve for this project. A half hour would be better, but then you can always have more retreat time tomorrow, and the next day.

At this quiet time, alone, but with your book in hand, come back again to this chapter. Re-read it. The contents are most important to you. Re-read it for greater conscious understanding and for greater subconscious impression.

Do this, and in the atmosphere of this retreat, you will have a revelation of the power and the willingness of your subconscious to support objective thinking and objective decisions. Your understanding of the subject will be clear and bright and your anticipation of desirable action will be positive and promising. You may have this kind of an experience at any time, with a subject of importance to you, by holding a personal retreat, like this one. This technique is recommended as "standard procedure for you in the control of self-influenced action.

⑨

A Trip into "Inner Space"

Do you have your ticket for that trip to the moon? Or do *you* prefer Mars?

There is a line beginning to form, you know, of people who see such a trip not only as a great adventure, but as a possibility that is becoming more reasonable each year. In fact a promotor wouldn't have too much trouble selling me a ticket, because I am just like you: I like adventure in my life. Furthermore, I don't intend to let any opportunity to *have* adventure pass me by. So perhaps I'll see you on one of those space ships, one of these days.

• Outer space is coming closer

Yes, a phrase that was new only a few years ago has come to be an everyday expression in our language. As laymen, we now speak about "outer space" in the same conversational casualness that we speak about the weather, or what happened at the office, or about the latest headlines. Outer space has taken more prominence in our conversation, of course, because science has begun to probe its vastness in efforts to learn some of the "secrets" of what is going on out there. The scientists are prompted by a growing awareness and importance of the effects of "outer space" on our lives. They seek knowledge that they believe will be the basis for greater understanding of the universe, and even beyond. They believe that this understanding could use, and even control, some of those forces in support of progressiveness on this earth of ours.

● Wonderful new horizons ahead

But as far as most of us are concerned, the net result of this scientific probing is that we are becoming more conscious of outer space. When we look "out there," we still see it as a big, beautiful "something." But we are now conscious of the probable existence of great forces out there and possibly of some kind of a great "plan," both affecting our earth. We have become more conscious of the fact that our earth is part of that plan—and not an isolated "us"—as compared to all the stars, and planets, and "what have you" out there. We have become conscious of the apparent fact that something important is happening that we have not been aware of before, that there are some "influences" out there that we should know more about. We are confident that scientists and adventurers will open up wondrous new horizons for us; in the meantime, the whole idea has become a fascinating, dramatic episode.

● A fascinating inner world

But while this intriguing "outer space" activity has been developing, another group of visionaries has been probing into "inner space." They have gone about it carefully and analytically. They, and the results of their work, haven't made the headlines like the "outer space" people have, even though theirs is really a much more dramatic story. Not only is the story of modern research into "inner space" more dramatic, but it affects each one of us in a much more personal manner than does the program of the "outer space" people. Yet there is a remarkable parallel between the story of "outer space" and that of "inner space." Both are concerned with something we cannot see. Both have a cause and effect basis that is related to our everyday lives. And both are related to great forces that do marvelous things, forces that are something like our concept of electricity. We know what electricity does, but very few know what it really is.

• Let's go into inner space

There is one significant difference between the forces that exist in "outer space" and those that exist in "inner space." Science has learned and displayed enough knowledge about the latter to enable people like you and me to control the forces of "inner space." "Inner space" is, of course, the human mind. Your mind is a wondrous world of "inner space," as remarkable and dramatic as is any concept you might have of "outer space." I invite you to take a "trip into inner space"—that inner space which is your mind—and learn what a miraculous world it is! And most remarkable, this will be a trip into your private world of "inner space," that mind which is yours alone.

You can imagine that an explorer of "outer space" would have a lot of equipment with him, primarily for observing and recording what happens on his trip. You will need to be similarly equipped for your trip to "inner space." However, you have this equipment at hand. All you need to do is be aware of its presence. You will "take" with you your intellect—which is your power to understand—and your emotions, or your power of sensing things by feelings. Now we are ready, like Alice in Wonderland, to step through the looking glass and, in imagination, leave this "outer world" and enter the "inner world" that is your mind.

• A bright, lively place

You don't find yourself in a dark, mysterious spot. Far from it. It's a light and lively place. There is a tremendous amount of activity. It isn't a noisy place, but there is an air of quiet efficiency and alertness. Your first impression is that you are in some kind of a complex control center. There is a big panel that holds several rows of what appear to be television screens. Several of these TV screens are showing "pictures." They are all different, as though each was tuned to a different station. Some seem to be showing much brighter, clearer pictures than others. Across "the room," a television *camera* is set up, and it is in operation, as though by remote control. Wires and cables seem to be everywhere. That this is a control center is confirmed by what you see in the center of "the room." There is a control panel, covered with switches, dials, and knobs. Operating that control panel is a figure that is a replica of you! This figure is intently watching the pictures that appear on those TV screens and he seems to be moving switches and knobs on the panel under the influence of what the screens show. That television *camera* is focused on this "you," recording everything you do and everything that those TV screens show.

• What controls this inner world

This is a very realistic picture of the control center in your mind. You will want to know what all of this represents in your real mind. Since we have used a "magic" touch to create this picture, we "pass the wand" again and bring forth a demonstration of the working of this control center. First, we will identify some of the working parts that you can see. Five of those TV screens are showing the reactions of the five senses of touch, sight, hearing, taste and smell. Several other screens have pictures when *parts* of your memory are working. The replica of you at the controls is really your will, that factor in your mind which decides what you shall do. Some of the wires represent the nerve canals and some of the cables represent veins and arteries. Now for the demonstration.

It is now late in the afternoon. According to those screens reflecting your emotions through the work of the five senses, you are hungry. This is understandable, because it is supper time. We put a plate of food in front of you. Immediately the screens showing sight and smell become bright and active. One of the other screens related to your memory shows what looks like a "commercial." It says: "You've seen things like this before. It's a meal! Eat and satisfy that hunger!" Your alert will observes the excited sight and smell screens and that particular "commercial" from a memory screen. Your will goes into action, turns knobs, throws switches. Nerves and blood cells are activated, your body reacts and you eat the food. As you do, the screens showing touch and taste become brighter and stronger.

You are seated with a companion as you eat. He talks to you, and the screen related to hearing comes on brightly. He asks: "Are you doing anything tomorrow night? How about coming over to our house?"

Your will knows there must be a response, so he looks for guidance to some of the other picture screens. One of the memory screens flashes a message, saying: "Your calendar is clear tomorrow." Another screen shows: "You like this person. You have enjoyed visiting him before." Based upon these messages, your will directs your response: "Thank you. I'll look forward to seeing you tomorrow."

• Your conscious mind in action

So much for the demonstration. Nothing too dramatic about it, was there? You are inclined to say that you know that this is about the way your mind works. You are right. You are somewhat familiar with this picture because this has been a demonstration of that part of your mental machinery called your conscious mind. This is the part of your mind that enables you to feel that sense of life and action that adds up to living as a human being. This is the part of mind that provides a constant sense of awareness in your life. In turn, you are aware of what is happening in your conscious mind.

The work that is done in your conscious mind is influenced by both your intellect and your emotions, as represented by the five senses. Your will causes you to act according to a combination of intellectual and emotional influences that are shown on those "screens" at any one time. However, this is only part of the demonstration. It was made as a necessary prologue to the second part, which is more than dramatic and which may, at first, seem almost unbelievable.

• The center of power in your mind

Now let's step through that doorway over there, and down these stairs, until we are in another center of activity, below the conscious mind. I should have told you to leave that emotional equipment you brought at the head of the stairs, because it will be of no use here. Only your intellect—your power to understand—has any value in this place.

Things are "all business" here. There isn't a soul in the place, yet a never-ceasing pattern of action exists. Some of our engineers are pretty proud of their development of "automation." They are really ages behind the times, because it has always existed in this part of the human mind. You have never been here before and you have never been emotionally aware of this part of your mind. You can't be emotionally aware of it. You can only be intellectually aware of its effects, as you are now and as you will always be from now on. You will see why this is so, and why it is so important, as we make a demonstration here.

• Be aware of this power

You can only be intellectually aware of the effects of this area because this is the non-conscious part of your mind, your unconscious mind. But a more direct term for you and me is the subconscious mind. You remember that we "walked downstairs" to get here, to the sub-conscious area. This is a perfect analogy to your real mind, since this area is below the level of your consciousness. You are neither consciously nor emotionally aware of it. But the most important factor in your life, from now on, will be your awareness of the effects of the work of your subconscious.

Remember that TV *camera* "upstairs"? Well, the screen that is showing the pictures being taken up there is down here! Remember those many extra screens, other than the "emotion" ones, that are up there? The controls that cause pictures to be flashed on those are also down here. And of course, many of the "cables" are connecting "upstairs" and "downstairs." That *camera* up there, you recall, is always taking a picture of what your will does, as well as everything that is shown on those screens. Thus everything that happens in your conscious mind, and everything that you do as the result of your will, is seen by that camera. Down below, everything that is recorded by that *camera,* is noted and filed away, permanently. This process began the moment you were born; it will continue for as long as you live.

● Values are measured subconsciously

What that *camera* records is automatically filed in your subconscious, according to the impression it makes as it is recorded,
as being of "minor" value, of "ordinary" value, as "important"
or as "noteworthy." Now, as we make the demonstration here,
all you have to remember is that everything you have ever done
or thought of consciously has been recorded and filed according
to the value your subconscious put upon it.

In the first part of our demonstration, we "magically" seat
you behind the wheel of your car. You are ready to drive off.
Upstairs, all of this is recorded on the "emotion" screens, is
taken in by that *camera* and is noted "down here." The picture
is "automatically" compared with the "files." It is found under
the "ordinary" heading; you have done this many times before.
There is pattern to be followed. This pattern is flashed onto
several of those extra screens upstairs, in the proper sequence.
Your will takes notes of these instructions and, apparently
"without thinking," you have the car in motion, driving down
the street. Things didn't go like this when you were learning
to drive, but eventually you repeated and repeated the right
motions until it seemed as though they were being done automatically. What did happen was that your subconscious recorded all of those repeated actions until it had a large "file" of
the same kind of reactions. It was a simple matter thereafter
for your subconscious to suggest to your will that you keep on
doing the same things whenever you got behind the wheel of
a car.

● Habits are subconsciously controlled

You don't drive your car "automatically." You act by reason
of habit, and habit is the result of prompting by your subcon-

scious to get you to repeat an action that matches a pattern previously filed away, subconsciously. You have scores of such subconscious habits. They govern most of what you do. They make life easier, or harder. They serve or defeat your purpose in life. They are all centered in this subconscious recording and filing center. Habit formation and control is a major function of the subconscious part of your mind.

For the second part of our "downstairs" demonstration, we are going to pull in one of those "agreements" you made with yourself in Chapter 2. Let's say it is the one about a belief of yours. At the time you made the choice, as I asked you to do, I believe that you had an emotional reaction. I hope you did because strong belief certainly is related to strong emotion. Anyway, that subconscious recording process was going on as you made that choice. IF you felt strongly about that choice, then it was filed under the heading of being "noteworthy," for the time being, at least.

• Noteworthy actions from noteworthy thoughts

Then, if you went about looking for an opportunity to demonstrate that belief within the time period I suggested, it is very likely that you made the demonstration and had a good experience from it. Why? Because of the "noteworthy" impression you made on your subconscious. As soon as an opportunity appeared, your subconscious was ready to say to your will: "Act! This is it!" Your subconscious tends to make you act effectively and enthusiastically when a "noteworthy" impression has been made upon you. This was so in the case of your belief, because you had established a positive attitude toward it through that "noteworthy" impression. Your subconscious wants you to transpose attitudes into action.

If you had resisted acting in response to that attitude, your subconscious would have decided that your choice wasn't noteworthy after all and it would have been filed under the "minor" heading. As a consequence, you would probably never act on it. On the other hand if you *had* acted that once—and had decided to act again in support of the same belief—your subconscious, with its growing file, would get ready to change that attitude to a habit. The recording and disposition of attitudes is another major function of your subconscious.

• Every experience labeled "positive" or "negative"

We will go "upstairs" and "outside" again in a moment. Before you go, take a quick look around at the labels on some of the "fiiles" here. Besides the "value" labels, there are countless other classifications. Habits and attitudes are classified as either positive or negative. Memories (there are hundreds of thousands of these) are classified as pleasant or unpleasant, useful or useless. There is just one file reference for some items; there are hundreds of references for others. Everything that you learned academically is stored here. Everything that you have learned through experience is on file.

• Your remarkable will

That's about it in this subconscious area. Let's go "upstairs." Before you leave the conscious mind area, however, take another good look at that replica of you that we call your will. Remember this fellow because we are going to call on him to do some remarkable things, which he can do. He can control to a great degree what that subconscious *camera* records, and he can largely control how great an impression a recording makes on the subconscious. This is most important to you, because if you can control what goes in, through the medium of your will, you've attained success. Because in that way you control what your subconscious puts out! The story of that control is ready for you in the next couple of chapters. Let's go "outside," where you can read, and let all of this "inner space" activity continue to do its work for you.

Outside now, take a look upward toward the sky. What's there? Outer space, the heavens, the stars and planets . . . vastness, great forces, something wonderful! But none of it is any more remarkable than where you have been, on this trip into "inner space." The "vastness" of your mind has nothing to do with physical size, of course. But when you couple the capacity of your conscious and your subconscious minds, you can conceive of almost limitless accomplishments in life. And now you know that "inner space" is a combination of great forces that are within you.

• Turn on your power

As remarkable as is our Creator's handiwork, as exemplified by our "outer space," His handiwork in designing "inner space" matches any of the "wonders" He has ever created. But it's up to you to use the power of your mind for all it's worth!

IN SUM

The subconscious contains the experience of life.

A major function of the subconscious is habit formation and control.

Another major function is the evaluation of experience.

A third is the recording and disposition of attitudes.

⊶ **RESULT-GETTING PROJECT** ⊷

There is both profound knowledge that is valuable to you and the promise of an exciting future in the contents of this chapter. All of the value of both should be yours, because they are potentially positive influences in your life. This value will be possessed by you if you have an intellectually complete, and an emotionally stimulating, reaction to the story of "inner space."

The project for this chapter, then, is to take it into retreat with yourself. The objective of this time in retreat is to bring the power that is within you, to live as you want to live, up to the point of action and use. This will come through a clear understanding of that power. This you will have, as the result of a retreat, and concentration on this chapter.

10

The Subconscious Mind:
a "Garden of Eden"
or a "Purgatory"

WHAT'S YOUR DREAM ABOUT AN IDEAL PLACE TO LIVE AN ideal life? Is it a South Sea island, or a villa on the Mediterranean, or a yacht cruising around the world? Everybody has such dreams, and they are pretty alluring when we find ourselves trapped by the pressure and routine of humdrum living.

But let me ask you a pertinent question. Why do you think that such an escape would take you to a "Garden of Eden" in your life? Is it not true that there would be compromises to life even on one of those idyllic South Sea islands? I believe that if you probe such dreams a bit, you would find that you really want to hold a "round trip ticket" so that you could come back if things didn't work out right.

I would not suggest that you abolish such dreams entirely. Better yet, look upon your fondest dream as an adventure that could come along and highlight your life. And it is entirely possible that this can happen, if you really want it to happen and you establish it as a goal!

• Escape from humdrum living

But escape from humdrum *everyday* living is another matter. You can do that without moving even a mile from your present environment. You can create a "Garden of Eden" of your own, right where you are now, by using the power of your mind for all it's worth!

You do want to use the power of your mind "for all it's worth," of course. In this, your book, you are in the process of developing the skill of so using it. Perhaps I appear to be a bit impertinent when I say that it is about time you decided to do this! But we are concerned here with that all-important item called "your life." The power of your mind has patterned your life in the past. How has this power done this patterning? What have the results been? How much skill has been related to the use of this power on your part? When I say "it is about time," it is a sincere, friendly observation, because that power has always been "turned on." It is "turned on" now, especially through that alert subconscious of yours. The point is that you can no longer afford to let this power go to waste, or be misused, or be directed toward non-constructive actions, not if you want to practice self-influence! How important this power is to self-control is obvious when you consider what can happen when it is uncontrolled. I am sure you will agree with me that "it is about time," for you!

For the next few minutes, keep that picture of your "trip into inner space" in focus. Especially recall that all-seeing eye that we described as a *camera* in your conscious mind and those voluminous *files* of what that camera has recorded in your subconscious mind. In this setting, we are going to make some more demonstrations of the power of your subconscious mind.

• Your habits on display

First we will analyze a couple of habits of yours. I will arbitrarily name them. As I do so, you might be inclined to raise your eyebrows and say: "How do you know that those are my habits?" I do not know for sure, of course, but I am choosing habits that have had priority in the lives of most people I have worked with, so I know I am not likely to miss you by very much. You won't have to go very far afield of my choices to find habits of yours that are parallel. Make that parallel choice on your own, if necessary.

The first habit in the spotlight is that of putting things off. Call it "rationalization," "procrastination," or anything you will. This is the action pattern in your life that makes accomplishment and achievement too rare in your life.

• Why you put things off

Just why do you put things off? There have been many times when your conscience has held up a warning signal, reminding you that it was morally wrong, or economically wrong, to act that way. But you still do it! Why? You do it, at this point in your life, because the power of your subconscious is influencing you to act this way! Recalling that we have defined the subconscious as your partner, you could be inclined to remark: "Well! that's a fine way for a partner to act!" I agree with you. That certainly is no way for a good partner to act, so it is about time you did something to bring this partner into line! There are two "keys" that I will give you in a moment that will open doors to a better partnership relations between you and your subconscious. Before you can use these keys effectively, you will need to know more about present conditions in that subconscious powerhouse of yours. So, let's return to that habit of putting things off.

You have always been able to give "reasons" for putting things off. You didn't have time, it was the wrong time, you were not "ready," you didn't feel like acting, the circumstances or the environment was "wrong." Those are typical of the "reasons" as you conjured them, even though the right term is "rationalizations." You were able to avoid acting, because in the conscious level of your mind, you do have a degree of control over that will of yours. As you know, that will is also affected by control from the subconscious. Actually there is no conflict here. Your will reacts to whichever influence is strongest in any situation; it reacts either to conscious or subconscious influence.

• Watch out for negative influences

Some time in your "history" you exerted that conscious influence that enabled you to put things off. That *camera* in your mind recorded those actions, and a *file* began to build up in your subconscious that put more importance on not acting. Soon the subconscious and the conscious influences were about equal, and it was "no trouble at all" to be able to put things off. Eventually that *file* grew so large that the subconscious influence became "automatic." And then it was just the "natural" thing to do, to put things off.

But there is much greater significance to this habit development than the fact that you permitted the power of your subconscious to become a negative influence. This negative influence of procrastination allowed other negative influences to appear and grow. Instead of those "on the surface" reasons that first prompted you to put things off, these other negative influences became the real reasons for this pattern in your life.

Fear took its place in the picture. Fear of acting progressively became a factor, because you *failed* to act consistently, so that lack of self-confidence became overpowering. And the expectation of no accomplishment came into the picture. You felt that you wouldn't succeed anyway, so why even start? These negative influences seemed to press in on you, as though you were surrounded by them, when the time came for you to act progressively.

• Lack of control brings fear

All of this, too, was recorded in your subconscious *files,* until eventually your subconscious was influencing you not to act because of fear and lack of self-confidence. "Lack of time" was no longer the real reason for putting things off. All of this is an example of effect of the power of your subconscious when it is not controlled by positive self-influence. An unpleasant picture? Yes, but it can be changed. But only by knowing that such negative conditions do exist—and how they came about—can you know what to change.

Now let's look at one other habit. This is the habit of nonparticipation. I am not implying that you are a confirmed "wall flower" in life, but I am referring to that area of activity in your life where you are more of a spectator than a participant. It could be in relation to your community life, your social life, your vocational life, or even your family life. You choose the area where you don't have that real sense of belonging that could come from a more active personal association. I am going to use community life as an example, but the same principle applies to any relationship situation in your life.

• Bystanders get no dividends from life

Why aren't you more of a participant in community life, since you really want to be? The answer can be traced back to a negative subconscious influence, that of the subordination of self-expression. Participation is dependent upon self-expression. In this case, a subconscious influence is insisting that the competition is too great for *your* self-expressed actions to have any value. Other people who are participants are too smart for you, and things are moving too fast! Subconsciously you are a spectator, so you act like one, passively!

However, you acquired this habit a bit differently than that "putting off" habit. This one probably had little conscious self-influence to start it off. It came about from outside influences that were recorded emotionally in your conscious mind; nevertheless they were picked up by your subconscious as important reactions. That competition is an example. You put a negative slant on it, even though you did not really know if this was justified, because you didn't test it by participation. Thus the whole energetic pattern of community life became a negative influence, an influence from the outside that allowed the power of your subconscious to build up. The same principle applies to the concept that other people are too smart for you, and that things are moving too fast. You let these outside influences become negative factors by not testing them. All of this is an example of uncontrolled outside influences being converted into negative subconscious influences. Unfortunately, this can happen too easily and comes from many sources. But the pattern can be changed and controlled.

• Habits acquired in two ways

Considering your life objectively, you know that you now have many habits that have been acquired by both of these processes. The two examples we used were negative habits. Obviously you have *many* positive habits, and they were acquired by either of these processes, also. That is, both your positive and negative habits were acquired either by some conscious effort to create them or by letting outside influences shape them in your subconscious.

We can bring these facts to a significant climax by putting one question before you. How much of the habit pattern you now have came about according to a conscious plan, and how much of it came about casually or accidentally? The answer would tell you exactly what kind of a life you have been leading up to this point, and it would describe the kind of a person you are. In some later chapters we are going to turn up that answer.

• Your life at the balance point

Just now, let's face the facts that have been revealed in this chapter. Your subconscious mind is the center of control of your life. At any one moment, whatever the balance point is between positive and negative subconscious influences, that's the kind of a life you are leading. The power of your subconscious mind is always turned on. Therefore, if there are more positive influences in action, your subconscious can be a "Garden of Eden" for you. If there are more negative influences in action, it certainly will be a "purgatory" for you.

Can you create and maintain a subconscious "Garden of Eden"? You can and you will, and I now give you the two "keys" that make this possible.

• Your Garden of Eden

The first one is: Deliberately control your conscious actions, keeping them on the positive side, so that they are recorded subconsciously as being "noteworthy."

The second one is: Change negative habit influences by deliberately and consciously cultivating positive habits that offset negative ones. Remember, you can't erase anything that is in your subconscious. You can't do away with a bad habit that is

recorded there. You can create and build up a substitute subconscious habit that will overpower the influence of a negative
one by recording the new habit as "noteworthy."

You will use these "keys" by first concentrating on the work
of your conscious will. This, in turn, will control what goes into
your subconscious. Deliberate control and change, using these
"keys," will inevitably make your subconscious the kind of a
partner you want to be, and the kind it should be.

Keep these "keys" handy. More . . . *more* . . . MORE is
just ahead where you will use them!

IN SUM

**Habits, good and bad, are acquired in two ways:
through your own conscious effort and through the
influence of outside factors.**

**You can deliberately control your conscious actions.
You can thus change the bad habits.**

---

o→ RESULT-GETTING PROJECT ←o

In this project, I want you to have an experience with
control of your conscious will. First, define and acknowledge one or two habitual actions of yours that are on the
negative side. Don't flinch from this suggestion. Such
habits have been acquired by you and you can't avoid
them by trying to deny their existence. You are not being
pilloried through this suggestion. What we are talking

about is something you don't want, and our objective is to get rid of it. Let me help you pick an example. This might have to do with a driving habit. Perhaps you have the habit of driving too close to the car in front of you. It doesn't make sense—and it doesn't get you there any faster—but still you drive that way, even if it is dangerous and discourteous. What would it take to get you to correct this habit, a stay in jail, revocation of your driver's license? That's pretty rough treatment and it probably would only make you resentful. No, the way to do it is to decide that you will drive at the proper distance and then consciously check your action based upon that decision. The point is that you must first consciously decide to do something else and thereby replace a negative action with a positive one. This is an example of deliberate conscious control of your action; if you do it, it will make you feel pretty good about yourself. You will prove that you can do the best thing, if you want to do it. But more than that, this deliberate conscious control is going to make a big impression on your subconscious, and eventually it will take over control of this new positive action, and make a new positive habit of it. This isn't as difficult to do as it sounds because such a change is a good change, and that is something you always want to be able to do. Prove to yourself that you can do it, by choosing an habitual negative action of yours and putting a bit of conscious control over it. As a result, what happens in your subconscious will make a "Garden of Eden."

11

The New Positive Concept
of Self-Control

How many times in your life have you signed your
name to an agreement that bound you to do something, or else?

Even though you put great value on your personal freedom,
and you would be wary of agreeing to do anything that would
jeopardize it, you have committed yourself to certain things
where a penalty was involved if you did not do them.

I'll name a few of the times you "signed your life away." You
have signed sales agreements, particularly when you made pur-
chases on a budget plan. Some of the fine print on those agreements bound you to an "or else" condition, yet you signed
them willingly! In your vocation, you may have signed con-
tracts that had all kinds of stipulations related to them, all of
them most binding. Even when you opened your bank account,
and applied for your insurance, you agreed to be bound by
certain specific conditions. Probably right now much of your
use of money, and your personal and vocational life, is influenced by such agreements. You signed your name to such bind-

ing agreements because it was the only way you could have or do what you considered necessary in your life.

• Sign your life away!

These are all agreements you have made with other people. But what about yourself? Have you ever made an agreement with yourself, to do something for yourself, or else? This is the most important kind of an agreement you can make, and I propose that you make one right now. This agreement involves not parts of your life, but rather your whole life, and I believe that you are ready for it.

You are ready now to understand a new creed of living. And you are ready to accept and adopt this creed. Self-influence has now assumed its rightful importance in your concept of the future. You are in a prime condition to effect control of your subconscious. You have been given the "keys" that will open the doors to that subconscious "Garden of Eden." All of this adds up to a new concept of living that can be defined in a "creed." Bind yourself to this new concept by asserting that it is your creed.

• A new creed of living

This is the creed of "do," the *positive* creed of action, performance, production and accomplishment. It is the opposite of the creed of "do not," the negative creed of rejection, procrastination, fear and failure.

This positive creed says "do, rather than do not"; "do, rather than talk about it"; "do, rather than wish"; "do, rather than wait."

Are you willing to embrace this creed? I am sure that it wouldn't take more than a little self-influence for you to do so. And I am sure that you are willing to say that your attitude toward it is that it is a good creed, and a right creed, for you. But like any creed, this one says a lot in a few words, so I want you to consider the "fine print" that is in back of those words before you go all the way and say it is your creed. Furthermore, I am sure you will agree with me when I say the acceptance of the creed should make a "noteworthy" impression on your subconscious mind. You will start out with a good attitude, of course, but the objective agreed upon should be to make this creed a good habit. So let's consider what is implied in the "fine print."

• Don't be normal

First of all, is this the creed of a normal person? Based upon your observation of others, you know that it is not! I can confirm your observation a hundred-fold. Very few of the thousands of people I have worked with in our courses and classes had such a creed before I worked with them. Yet they all considered themselves pretty normal persons. Like these people, when they eventually adopted the creed, you are going to have to accept another designation than normal. Yes, if you adopt it you are going to have to accept the designation of an unusual, an abnormal person. For you will be a person who has veered away from the normal track and from living the typical, ultraconventional life. You will be a person who is always on the productive, progressive track, and *that* is *abnormal!*

Secondly, you are going to have to discard any ideas about travelling in the middle of the road. You are going to definitely take one side, the positive side. No one is ever able to take a middle of the road stand anyway. He has to be on one side or other, and if he doesn't voluntarily make a choice, he is pushed to one side or the other, or pushed off the road. You are going to boldly take the positive "right" side and never veer over to the negative "left" side.

• Be above normal

And third, you are not going to be able to live moderately, if such has been your interpretation of the "safe" way. The person who is living abnormally, and boldly travelling on the side of the road of his choice, is not living moderately. Moderation too often means appeasement and compromise. You can't compromise with this "do" creed, so you are going to have to live immoderately!

This "do" creed, then, means that you will live abnormally, or above the normal. You will travel only on the positive side of the road of life. You will live immoderately, by going "all the way." Knowing the true significance of this creed, are you now willing to ally yourself with it?

You have not the slightest reason to be hesitant about your decision. This is the creed of a person who has established his own importance to himself. But there is still another vital reason for its being your creed. The creed of "do" is made up of the kind of stuff that makes subconscious self-influence clear and certain. You will have the highest score of "noteworthy" impressions on your subconscious by acting according to the creed. The creed will make your subconscious the kind of a partner you want it to be.

Are you adopting the creed? You are, so say "yes"! Say it aloud, so that conscious will of yours blinks a bit from the reverberations and so that your affirmation is recorded on that *subconscious camera* as the brightest impression ever!

• Put a plus sign on yourself

Probably to you, as it has been to most people, all of this is a new concept of self-control. It IS the modern concept, the needed concept in today's world. The emphasis is on "doing" for self-control. It puts a plus sign on action. This plus sign brings into focus those positive terms of *forward, increase, reinforce* and *progress*. It negates the outmoded and negative "do not" concept of self-control, with its minus sign on action. That is the concept that puts undue importance on the negative terms of *retardation, want but can't have, ultra-moderation* and *withdrawal.*

Actually this apparently new concept did not mushroom up overnight. It has been a long time coming to this usable climax. From a psychological standpoint, it has a background of years of testing and development in the Simmons Institute and years of research and confirmation in the world of science. The years of experimentation are over. The time of practical application is here. Thus it is a new concept, but one which has been tried and tested by thousands of persons, and which has been stamped "approved" by them. Their approval means that you can have confidence in its practical application to your life.

• This is the turning point

With the adoption of this positive creed, you have reached a mid-point climax in your experience with self-influence. This is the turning point, where well-grounded *planning* has made you ready to step into the *practice* period. You are well armed with a set of plans that have been custom made to fit you and your life.

I believe that a brief restatement of your planning steps is in order here, in recognition of your accomplishments to this point. First, you prepared yourself for this experience by making those three "agreements" with yourself, in Chapter 2. By now, you have made the demonstrations required of those agreements and have thus established your own importance to yourself. This created the initial positive attitude toward self-influence. By the way, you have made those demonstrations, haven't you? Or do I have to remind you again that there was a vital preparatory action inherent in that step?

• Follow through on your creed

To be truthful with yourself, you can't adopt that creed unless you have followed through on your agreements, can you? If you did not follow through, you were subscribing to that negative "Do not" creed and your subconscious mind was so conditioned. If you haven't followed through, do so now. It's never too late to overpower a negative experience with a positive one. You know that!

Then you progressed in your planning to a rather long list of items in Chapter 4. You made your choices and determined what you could do about each one. You wrote all this down on the important piece of paper that is now serving as a bookmark for that chapter. (You can see just the edge of that paper exposed in your book, can't you? Better be sure it is there or you will be taking the "wind out of the sails" of your creed!)

Then, in the last chapter, you acquired those two "keys" to subconscious self-influence, the "key" of deliberately controlling your conscious actions so that best impressions are made in your subconscious and the "key" of deliberately substituting positive habits for negative ones.

• New attitudes—new habits

And then, finally, in this chapter, you accepted the creed that was the crowning climax of your planning. You have noticed, I am sure, that every step in this planning phase was based upon the positive action concept. Other than to provide you with a framework upon which to build a finished product through self-influence, there was another specific purpose in this emphasis on "do, positively." All along the way, I have been *suggesting* that you accept this concept. By doing things in the planning steps, you have been suggesting to yourself that you accept them. You have accepted them, and that supports the secondary purpose of the steady emphasis on "do, positively." This has created a positive attitude within you, within your subconscious mind. The objectives just ahead are to convert that positive attitude into positive habits, everyday, lifelong habits.

The cultivation of this positive attitude has been a "noteworthy" accomplishment, by yourself, for yourself. This, as I said, is the turning point, from planning to practice. But the planning must have carry-over into the practice steps for the latter to have real meaning in your life. You can insure this carry-over by putting your subconscious to work on the importance of this planning. You can do this simply and effectively, and you can do it tonight, assuming that some of the night hours are your regular sleeping hours. You can do it just as effectively if your regular sleeping hours are during daylight. The point is that the beginning and end of your regular sleeping time set the stage for this relationship with your subconscious.

• Tonight is the night!

Here I am going to assume the direct role of a "teacher" and ask you to do the following as though it were an assignment you would accept without question.

Tonight (or today), just before you are ready to go to sleep (and preferably after you are in bed and ready to turn the light out), re-read this whole chapter. This is Chapter 11. The title is "The New Positive Concept of Self-Control." Re-read it all, just before "lights out" tonight. As you read and come to that reference to your list in Chapter 4, pause a moment to re-read that list, too. When you have finished with the chapter, (tonight), place a bookmark at the beginning of this chapter and turn out the lights!

Tomorrow morning, as soon as possible after you awaken, re-read this chapter again (and include the "list," also). Re-read it no later than breakfast time. Then put the book aside, and go about the day's activities.

• Tomorrow will be bright

During tomorrow, and the days that immediately follow, you will constantly have a clear, bright picture in your conscious mind of all of the pertinent details of your plans! During the hours that you read the next chapters in your book, you will consciously relate every clear detail of your plans to the practice steps, as though they have a natural affinity for each other. This clear picture in your conscious mind will be kept in focus there because your subconscious mind was greatly impressed during this "sleeping hour" program of re-reading this chapter.

For the moment, don't ask why this will happen, just do it! (I won't let you down. You will know why a bit later.) Just do as I suggest and let this manifestation of subconscious self-influence *happen to you.*

• Stop here and enjoy life

If you want to make this a truly memorable experience, don't read beyond this chapter until after tonight, until after you have completed this assignment. I will admit that this sounds a bit presumptuous, telling you not to read more in your book, for the moment. But I want you to step from the planning stage to the practice stage with the greatest possible anticipation of great accomplishment ahead for you. This pause, and this sub-conscious conditioning, will heighten your anticipation, and bright-eyed anticipation is "good medicine" for anybody!

IN SUM

Make an agreement with yourself to accept a new creed of living.

This you will do by adopting a positive attitude toward action and progress.

o⭢ RESULT-GETTING PROJECT ⭠o

The project for this chapter has already been assigned, but here I want to put emphasis on the part that is covered in the last paragraph of the chapter. Don't read beyond this chapter until after you have completed the whole project. This is your first experience with the power of your subconscious serving you while you sleep. To be effective, it must be a complete experience, without distracting influences. So please stop at this point and have this experience.

12

Science and the Subconscious Mind

CONTROL OF THE POWER OF THE SUBCONSCIOUS MIND!

Is it really possible for a lay person like yourself, or does it require the services of a professional expert?

Is it a legitimate theory with scientific backing, or is it just an idea of a few dreamers?

Is it a proven proposition, or is it still in the experimental stage?

If you did not have questions like these in your mind, I think you could be considered among the group that P. T. Barnum said were "born every minute." Perhaps at some time you have been a "sucker" for some illegitimate deal that sounded wonderful at the time. If you have, then you have learned that you should always examine the validity of any program that appears to have mystery or "magic" as its basis. Certainly, control of the subconscious could seem to have those attributes, and, therefore, your questions are most timely.

• Get the answers! Know the facts!

In fact, I wanted you to have these questions. That is the reason I left the big "why" hanging in mid-air in the last chapter when I asked you to perform an unusual exercise with "no questions asked." I am sure that the act only emphasized the question, so I will confess that it was done deliberately. A bit of rather strong "outside influence" was put into play there, wasn't it? But I assure you that it was a positive influence, aimed at creating a desire on your part for some facts. Since supplying these facts involves delving into the scientific aspects of self-influence, I don't want the "answers" to have an abstract tone to them. Fresh from that recent experience of yours, you will be able to read this chapter with the same personal feeling for it that you have had all along.

• The role of science in society

Science has three major functions in its relationship to the society of mankind. First, its function is to gather knowledge of facts and laws concerning anything and everything that affects our world and its people and to evaluate the knowledge through observation and reasoning. Explanations that come through this function are "theories."

Secondly, the function of science is to convert usable theories into practice, or to help convert them and apply them. This function is considered to have a three-way application: 1. to the natural sciences, such as chemistry and physics; 2. to the social sciences, such as economics, sociology, medicine; 3. to the applied sciences, such as engineering and agriculture. This function might be called the professional application of science, where extensive preparation, training and experience are needed in the use of scientific theories.

• Lay people apply science

The third function of science is to interpret scientific theories and to demonstrate the possibility of their use by lay people (such as you) to the extent that scientific knowledge may be used in everyday living, where practicable. In this area too, preparation, training and experience are necessary to apply scientific theories properly. But here we take advantage of what has been done professionally and make a streamlined easy-to-understand application, related to a specific need.

In this chapter, we are going to refer to the first two functions, but we are going to concentrate on that third function. And where we refer to the professional field of science, we will be mostly concerned with the social sciences. Incidentally, let's clear up another point before we go any further. This concerns the word "theory." Theory is not a "bad word," as is so often thought by the average person. A theory is really an explanation based upon thought, observation and reasoning. It is a scientific principle, stated so as to have common understanding. In this chapter we are not referring to just good ideas that might or might not work, we are referring to scientific theories that have been tried and tested professionally and eventually related to that third function of science, the interpretation to lay people. We are not talking about theory versus practice as though they were opposed to each other. We are talking about practice based on scientific theory, which is the best kind of "practice" to rely upon.

• Science is part of your life

There are many examples about your life and in your life where this three-step scientific process is influencing you. Our national and community public health programs are good examples. Public health is a basic need for community health, of course. But each of us has come to depend upon such a program to help raise the level of our individual expectations of health and long life. However, there first had to be established that "1-2-3" scientific process in relation to health, before the program could affect individuals.

Knowledge from research (Step 1) had to be transposed into professional application (Step 2). But until the application by lay people (Step 3) was included, the program could not be called a *public* health program. As a consequence, you and I are practicing the principles of good public health every day. We understand the *use* and the *benefits* of these principles, even though we are non-professional lay people.

• Lay people cause scientific progress

Our broad program of general education is another example. Research has included methods and techniques of teaching, as well as educational programs. Professional application now extends practically throughout the human life-span, from nursery school to unlimited adult education programs. But here again, Step 3 in the scientific process is most significant. Outside of the formal educational program, there are many more lay people interpreting and using good educational principles than there are professional people. This has broadened the base of our educational program immeasurably.

For example, in our Sunday schools, in group-work social programs, in business and industry, even in our homes, there are thousands and thousands of teachers, all lay people. All are effectively using the principles of good education that originated in Steps 1 and 2. Indeed, a large part of our culture and economy is dependent upon this army of lay teachers of which you undoubtedly are, or have been, a "member."

• More lay scientists needed

The subject of your book, "the power of the subconscious mind," is another example of the same 3-step scientific process, except that it has not yet had the full impact that it should have. The teamwork of researchers, professional and lay people has been effective in public health and in education for such a long time that we have come to take the relationship for granted. But in the relationship to the power of the subconscious, while research and professional application have reached a high level of effectiveness in modern times, lay interpretation and use of the proven principles have unfortunately lagged.

There are probably several reasons for this. One, the absorption of a new concept, even if it is good, is a slow process in the normal mass of people. Two, there has been an air of undue mystery about this field. And, three, the use of this "power" requires some preparation, training and experience; as yet, too many people seem reluctant to participate under that premise. All of this is most unfortunate, because there could be the same kind of interpretation and use here by people as a whole as, for example, with public health and education.

• Apply scientific principles yourself

However, these reasons do not affect you, since the major purpose of your book is for you, under your own "steam" as a lay person, to bridge the gap in the field of "the power of the subconscious" between research and professional application and its application to your own life. Besides, you have already been a participant in the preparation you have done so far through your book. What you are doing is preparing yourself through knowledge, relating yourself to training under my guidance and with your book and bringing some first-hand experience into your life, in relation to the "power of the subconscious." This, in the "1-2-3" scientific process, amounts to the realistic application of Step 3 to your life.

While most of the research and professional application in this field has been in modern times, individuals recorded their observations and reasoning about the subconscious a long time ago. Before the turn of the century, Sigmund Freud advanced some theories that are credited with being the conception of psychoanalysis. Included in Freud's reasoning was the famous "repression theory" in which he explained the unconscious or subconscious mind as the place where taboo impulses were banished, only to cause unfavorable influences which inflict themselves upon individuals. Alfred Adler, a follower of Freud, disagreed with some of his reasoning. Adler observed that man had a tendency to let social conditions over-rule him and thwart his desires. Subconsciously, according to Adler, man rebels against this outside pressure and tries to overcome his "inferiority." Adler said that this rebellion is based upon fundamental urges for self-expression and recognition.

• Research is the basis for this knowledge

Other researchers followed the lead of these two men, and doors to the power of the subconscious began to open. Professional application of the developing theories began to be more wide-spread. A few people even took the practice of the theories into the Step 3 area, notably the French psychiatrist, Coué, with his famous "every day in every way I'm getting better" program. At the time, this was generally thought to be a "novel" idea. It was an actual program of the use of subconscious self-influence, under guidance, and skeptics had to admit there were many demonstrations of its effectiveness.

As modern-day research and professional application began to work hand in hand, knowledge and results produced some of the proven theories that are related to the principles of your book. Among these is the fact that the conscious and the subconscious are not separate "minds" or separate functions but are part of one mind, and they are completely interdependent. Another fact that has been proved is that no one inner or outer influence is predominate in human life; rather, there are several basic urges, existing and working together. Obviously you have seen that these two facts are prominent factors in this book.

• Professional use of subconscious influence

Significant scientific developments in the fields of medicine, education and social welfare, paralleling the interest in the subconscious, eventually came to a converging point with the realization that the subconscious was a major key in determining what a person did and what his reactions were to environmental influences. Medical doctors accepted the fact that recovery from serious illness or injury was largely dependent upon the patient's state of mind, that is, his conscious and subconscious reaction to his circumstances. Hypnotism, long a mysterious "something" with theatrical overtones, became a tool of the profession; the influencing of the subconscious through medical hypnosis is now ethical practice.

• Modern knowledge is the basis of this book

Educators "modernized" many of their techniques, putting more emphasis on "desire" for learning than on compulsion.

"Desire," in this case, was related to those fundamental, sub-consciously supported urges. Interest in education blossomed after that. Floyd L. Ruch, professor of psychology at the University of Southern California, characterized this concept in his popular text, *Psychology and Life.* He states that "learning is a changing of the individual's way of responding." Again it is obvious that we have included this modern reasoning in this book.

Scholars and administrators in the fields of social welfare and human behavior have come to adopt programs that are based upon appealing to the subconscious and those fundamental urges. They have learned that the success of any program that affects people is dependent upon individuals who want to participate, from way down inside, and upon the opportunity to satisfy those urges.

All of these modern-day interpretations of the power of the subconscious are generally based upon the theory of "action psychology," whose development is credited to Professor William Jones. Professor Jones' theory is that everything we do is based upon conscious action that is consistently motivated by influence. And certainly that is the theory of this book.

• We are partners with scientists

As we become participants through Step 3, and take our rightful places in that scientific trilogy as it relates to the power of the subconscious, we do so with the knowledge that the groundwork has been laid in Steps 1 and 2. We become partners in this action in the same way that we are partners in the programs of public health or education. We participate as individuals, using proven principles. But we will never consider "stepping over the line" to assume the prerogatives of professional people in this field. Where we need medical help, we will get it. Where we need professional psychological or psychiatric guidance, we will seek it. And we will depend upon professional research and application to set the stage for our personal applications in this field. By participating in Step 3 with this attitude, you and I are availing ourselves of all of the advantages of the groundwork that has been laid, and we intelligently shun "trial and error" or queer ideas.

• Answer your questions

Now, with this background of the scientific basis of your book and its contents, you are in a better position to understand the answer to the "question" left hanging in air at the end of the last chapter.

During the earlier years of the research-application development of knowledge of the subconscious, some unusual phenomena were observed. For example, during a particular experiment, a group of children were "talked to" while they slept. While their conscious minds and bodies were at rest, that is, while they were sleeping, researchers audibly spoke to each individual child. As they talked, they made suggestions to the children that they do certain things after they awoke. The experiment, with the same suggestions, was repeated for several nights and the children observed during their waking hours. Soon it was noted that the children were responding to the subconsciously imposed suggestions. They began to act in the manner suggested to them. The acts were all simple in nature and related only to things the children would normally want to do.

• Part of you never sleeps

This and subsequent experiences eventually revealed that the time in which the conscious part of the mind is at rest is excellent for inducing progressive activity in the subconscious part. That this must be done by deliberate suggestion was proved as research and application continued. An interesting, down-to-earth application was made to two groups of Navy trainees during World War I. Both groups were being taught the Morse Code. One group was taught exclusively by the conventional classroom method. The other group had the classroom teaching supplemented by continued audible instruction while they slept. The startling result was that the group who were subconsciously influenced during their sleeping hours learned the code in about one-quarter the time required for the other group! Since then, similar applications have been used effectively in other academic areas, notably in the teaching of languages.

Most significant, however, has been the application of this technique to psychological and medical therapy. Incidental to all of this has been the observation in the field of psychology that people need to train, guide and control their emotions, desires and habits. We agree with that theory, of course, as evidenced in this book. Beyond the conscious guidance of ourselves through self-influence, the findings of professional people indicate that emotional and habit training is greatly stepped up by supplemental influence while we sleep. In a survey of many applications of this sleep-learning technique, as reported in the journal of the American Psychological Society, the consensus of opinion was that the technique was much more effective in the emotional field than in the academic field. Hence our interest in this valuable technique.

• 24-hour use of subconscious power

The reason that this "sleep time" influence is effective is because action within the subconscious is best generated when your body is at rest, when tension has been relieved, when you are in a position to let this power be generated. The project that was suggested to you in the last chapter was effective because you instigated that self-influence experience at the time when your subconscious was free of all other obligations. Thus your subconscious was able to concentrate on the project you had assigned to it.

• You are a psychologist

Now, just one more item while we are talking about "science." This has to do with the word "psychology." Psychology is as "old as the hills" or, rather, as old as the human race. All that we moderns have done is put an official name on the field of knowledge of why people act, think and feel as they do. We have rightly elevated that field to the status of a science, and we call it psychology. You are a practicing psychologist, on the layman's level. You always have been and always will be. How good a practitioner you have been is another question. How good you will be is pretty well plotted, isn't it? Don't back away from the words "science" and "psychology." Claim them as the background for your experience with subconscious self-influence.

So now, "practicing psychologist," we have come to a good time to talk about how to use the power of your subconscious.

IN SUM

The major purpose of this book is to instruct you in applying scientific knowledge to the influence of the subconscious.

Action is best generated in the subconscious when your body is at rest.

ᐁ RESULT-GETTING PROJECTS ᐊ

Since this chapter is essentially an academic presentation, I have set up a little quiz covering the contents. The questions emphasize the salient points in the chapter and the answers you find for them will prove to you that the basic theories regarding the power of your subconscious are sound and approved. I think such a testimonial is important to you. This is not an "examination." Re-read any part of the chapter if you cannot answer a question offhand.

1. There are three major functions in science. Where do you fit into those functions?

2. Where and when in your daily life do you benefit from your participation in the work of science?

3. What is the basic theory upon which the modern-day interpretation of the subconscious mind and its functions are based?

4. Why can the subconscious be called upon while you sleep, and how?

5. Why did that experience you had with the project in Chapter 11 have the effect upon you that it did?

13

How to Use the Power
of Your Subconscious

HOW MANY TIMES, IN THE MOST RECENT YEARS OF YOUR
life, have you experienced a sense of power? Not often enough,
I venture to suggest, and then it probably was a vicarious experience. You can remember *moments* of having this feeling
of power from the time you were a youngster. Memories of
those earlier years include times when you skated, rode a bike,
a coaster wagon or a sled and you pushed yourself until you
were going faster and faster. For a moment or two, your speed
would be so excessive that you were just on the edge of being
scared. But, my, what a sense of power it gave you!

• A new kind of personal power

Such moments had more grown-up flavor to them in your
'teen years. Perhaps the sense of power came when you shot

a rifle for the first time, or when you were the starring participant in competitive games, when you were the "big" sister or brother to some "little kids."

All of these incidents came from environmental opportunities, a sense of power coming from the outside. There was no lasting quality to it. A transition of this kind of power to adult years is sought by some people, but it is nothing to be recommended. Some people, for example, get behind the wheel of a car and induce a momentary sense of power by seeing how high they can push the speedometer and get away with it. The feeling of power fades as the car slows down. No one is entitled to this kind of power. However, everyone seeks some sense of personal power, because it is a form of recognition of ourselves. There is a kind of personal power you should seek in acknowledgment of your importance to yourself.

• You have used this power at times

As an adult, you have already had some manifestations of this kind of power. You may not have sought it because you didn't know how, but each time it came to you, it had a lingering, desirable after-effect. And each time it came, it came from within you, not from the outside.

If you are a mother, this sense of power came to you at the birth of your child. You had the feeling that you had surpassed any other accomplishment in your whole life by being an instrument of the ultimate in creativeness. The power of creativeness gave you a transcending feeling of personal power.

Perhaps, like thousands of men and women, you have had religious experiences that have caused a welling up of courage and strength within you. Perhaps, like many others, you are able to renew this sense of personal power consistently.

There have been times when the acquiring and the possession of knowledge has given you that sense of inner power. These have been times when specific knowledge has made you better prepared and more confident in the face of a specific requirement in life. Sense of power from this source is inherent in your experience with this book.

And there should have been times in your life when a sense of power came because of the effect of your influence on other people. We have already discussed the existence of negative power by which some persons usurp the lives of others. You, of course, have never been, or ever will be, a supporter of this kind of power. But there have been times, I am sure, when your influence has powerfully and positively affected the lives of others and you have rightfully felt that inner, personal power.

• This power was demonstrated just yesterday

Your "biography" would undoubtedly record many such manifestations of feeling this inner sense of power; if your personal history is up-to-date, it will record that you had such an experience just yesterday and that you are still feeling the effects of it. Just yesterday (if you have been faithfully using your book as a guiding light), you made that demonstration to yourself of the effectiveness of your subconscious in creating a positive attitude. Today you have a clear, bright picture of your plans, which gives a sense of readiness to put them into action. This readiness gives a sense of power, the power to act, the power over circumstances and environment, as these might affect your plans. This power came from within you. It was created through the work of your subconscious and it is maintained as a feeling of power by your subconscious.

• Only one source of inner power

The same basic pattern that covers your experience of yesterday and today covers all of the experiences you have had with the feeling of inner power. The feeling of power seemed to well up from nowhere. In each case there was action involved, but it was all physical or mechanical conscious action, intrinsically resembling many other actions in your life which did not bring on this sense of power. You didn't press a button and suddenly have this power turned on! There is no such button that anybody can press. You can't force this power to appear. You can only let it appear, after you have set the stage with proper conscious preparation. Only the power of your subconscious can bring this desired feeling of inner power to you.

Was this as true with the other experiences in your life as it was with the one you were guided into yesterday? The answer is "yes." With a mother, the physical preparation of pregnancy and the physical act of giving birth are overtoned by her love and anticipation of the coming child. This love and anticipation grows as her period of pregnancy advances. Her subconscious mind is anticipating the birth as well as is her body. With the child finally in her arms, her subconscious lets that love literally overflow and turns that anticipation into fulfillment. Without that subconscious preparation, the birth *could* be as emotionally devastating as it is physically arduous. The power of the sense of fulfillment was already within her, subconsciously. She had only to let it be felt.

• Inner power from knowledge

The acquiring of knowledge, of course, is related to books, classes, courses or experience. Possibly only a relatively small portion of what you have learned through these processes has given you a feeling of power. When it did happen, it was not the "facts" that you had learned that in themselves gave you this feeling; it was the personal use you related them to. It happened when you related them to a goal or objective and particularly when you anticipated the use of them during the learning process. It happened when you were motivated to learn by saying to yourself: "These facts, in my possession, will enable me to do a certain something better." Thus, while the memory "departments" of your subconscious were helping you assimilate the facts, other "departments" were remembering your high anticipation of their use. With the facts acquired, your subconscious played back that anticipation in the form of satisfying accomplishment and that sense of personal inner power.

• Strength from inner power

So it is with church attendance, or with prayer. These acts seem to bring about passive reactions. But the repetitious relationship with them also conditions your subconscious mind. When, at some time in your everyday life, you have the need for courage and strength beyond the normal, your subconscious will remind you that the source of this courage and strength lies in your faith. Your subconscious was storing up this inner power so that you could feel it at the time you needed it most.

And so it is in your relationships with others. When you act to be of service to others, those subconsciously stored traits of graciousness and understanding influence your actions. Your subconscious intentions are of the best and the other person responds accordingly. The fact that your influence affects another person gives you a sense of personal power, but it comes about only because of the release of that positive subconscious power to act graciously and with understanding.

• How to turn on inner power

There is one fundamental difference between experiences such as these and the recent one concerning your plans. It is that the latter was done with great deliberateness, with one hundred per cent predetermination of the results! And that is the secret of using the power of your subconscious, by deliberate preparation and by conscious predetermination of the outcome. Beyond that, you do nothing; you can do nothing to cause its power to be a major factor in your life. And this brings us to the first and only time we shall consider anything like a "formula" or "rules and regulations."

I did not dream up this formula. Science did not invent it, although science can be credited with discovering it. When the Creator gave you that two-part mind of yours—the conscious and the subconscious—He made this formula "part and parcel" of the fact that you are a human being. The formula has three steps to it.

1. Deliberately condition your subconscious by what you do consciously. You are always aware of what you are doing. Apply a personal "golden rule" to this awareness. "Do unto your subconscious as you would have your subconscious do unto you." That is why the recording *camera* is in your mind.

2. Wholeheartedly want the best results from such self-influence action. Certainly this supports the creed of "do" that is now yours. This is why that priority "filing system" exists in your subconscious.

3. Let your subconscious have free reign in demonstrating its power. Let things happen to you and they will happen to you. That is why you have your will at the control panel in your mind.

The use of this formula will bring the power of your subconscious mind into full play. It is the only way to use it positively, and the word "positive" is the only thing that I would add to this formula. Of course, I don't know why anyone would want to be deliberate about negative conditioning, or would want, or let, negative outcomes be predominate, least of all you!

• Go on a retreat to start right

Now we can add some practical "do it yourself" suggestions to this formula. You have heard of the "retreat" program that many churches have. Perhaps you have had the remarkable experience of attending one. In such an experience, a person spends many consecutive hours in silent contemplation with himself and the spirit of his Creator and, in a practical fashion, with his subconscious. The objective is for him to see himself, and his life, objectively. Frankly, the best way to make steps one and two of the formula most effective is to go to a "retreat" in preparation for them. The time you spend alone, if only a few minutes, in contemplation of deliberate action will start you off on the right track without the slightest doubt. Try to establish a pattern of brief but regular "retreats" in your daily life.

• Avoid trial-and-error ideas

Don't use the trial-and-error method of finding the right material for your subconscious to work on. There is no need for you to do it. This pattern of action is a time and effort waster and unnecessarily delays achievement. Seek guidance, if you are uncertain of the best steps to take at any time. Books, courses, counseling, the experience of others are all resources for supplying yourself with usable knowledge. With such proven knowledge, you will follow the positive course of self-influence.

Your subconscious is a versatile powerhouse. It can, and is willing to, work on many actions and results at the same time. Give it the chance to work for you at its top capacity by having a variety of positive actions on your program at any one time. In fact, the more you use the power of your subconscious, the more it will appear to be a power in your life. Before you are through with your book, you will realize that here is one certain instance where practice makes perfect.

• Be positive! Be deliberate!

Deliberate guidance, positive guidance, is the key to using the power of your subconscious. The best use of this power is dependent upon this guidance. So strongly do we believe in this, at the Simmons Institute, that we guide students of our home study course into the ultimate in deliberate, positive self-guidance. We provide them with the tools for the guided influence of their subconscious minds, while they sleep. This guidance is directly related to the subject matter of the course. This is an extension of the type of experience you had, in relation to Chapter 11 of your book.

• Use your tireless subconscious

You know now, of course, that this is possible because the subconscious mind does not sleep . . . does not need sleep. You know that it is willing to be influenced while you sleep. Because we help our students take advantage of this, their relationship with the course is stepped up immeasurably. Like them, I know you will take advantage of every opportunity offered you in the practice steps to increase the power of your subconscious, by influencing it while you sleep.

IN SUM

The secret of using the power of your subconscious lies in deliberate preparation and conscious predetermination of the outcome.

You must deliberately condition your subconscious.

You must wholeheartedly want the best results.

You must allow your subconscious to have free reign in demonstrating its power.

o→ RESULT-GETTING PROJECT ←o

Let the power of your subconscious cause positive action, now. Turn back to Chapter 4. The important piece of paper that has been marking that planning chapter was made up according to the formula given in this chapter. It is a prime example of deliberate preparation, and conscious predetermination, and it was entirely self-influenced. Now take those plans in hand and consider what action on them will mean to you. It will mean a positive, progressive experience for you. It will mean that you will be doing the best things for the best results. It will mean accomplishment through a self-influenced plan. Have you ever had a greater, more constructive sense of power, than is coming from this knowledge of what you have done, on your own, and what you can do, on your own? The power of your subconscious is the source of this conscious feeling of power; now you know how to get it whenever you need it!

14

The Subconscious Mind and Your Past

You have a past—AND WHETHER YOU ARE PROUD OR unhappy about parts of it—*every* part of your personal history is permanently engraved like carving in rock. You can't erase what is recorded, and certainly you can't go back and live your life over again with the idea of making a revision in your history.

If some demanding authority were to tell you to display all of your recorded history, to lay it all out so that it could be analyzed and criticized, would you flinch from the thought? It *could* be a distressing experience—since everything is recorded, the good as well as the bad—couldn't it?

But you need have no fears, because, with the exception of a psychoanalyst whom you would trust, no one can order you to take stock of your past, except yourself! This is so because the only place where the *complete* history of you is recorded is in your subconscious, and you well know that your subconscious is a private world of your own.

• Your past has great value

I am about to ask you to display all of your past history completely and objectively, but I assure you that it will be a private session, and a rewarding one. Let's first consider the reasons for having this unusual experience.

In the practice of subconscious self-influence—the new skill which is about to have a "trial run" in your life—you are dealing with the most outstanding subject in the world, your own life. Everything that you do in the practice steps will directly affect your life. As you reach that promised point of perfection in self-influence, *every moment* of your life will be affected by this concept of living. In other words, you are reaching the point where a predetermination of the fundamental pattern of your whole future is possible. Certainly this holds out the promise of a good life, the kind of a life you want.

• Is life a privilege, or a responsibility?

This kind of a lifetime, under the star of positiveness, is one of the privileges accorded the person who is skillful in self-influence. But with privilege, always comes responsibility. With the privilege of "calling your own shots," and leading a self-influenced life, you must also accept the complete responsibility for your own life. This is a tremendous responsibility, affecting the most valuable thing in the world, as far as you are concerned.

There is no doubt of your ability to meet this responsibility, but since you are placing yourself in a position to be primarily accountable for your own life, I feel that I would not be meeting my responsibility if I failed to call some facts to your attention.

• Consider your whole life

In this and the next two chapters, we are going to be concerned with your whole life, as opposed to segments of it. And we will be concerned with you in the sense of the whole person. You will recall that we talked about the "latest models" in human beings in Chapter 7. You were encouraged to make the obvious choice of one of the models as an ideal for yourself. Here you took a quick "look-see" at the whole life and the whole person. NOW our objective is to enable you to take full responsibility for the achievement of that ideal and to assure yourself that every individual action will support and complement your whole life and your whole person.

To do this we are first going to "turn around" and look at the past. Then you will turn once again and look at the present. And finally, you will face forward and look into the future. Each "turn" will prove that your interpretation of your responsibility for your life is directly related to self-influence and your subconscious mind. As we step from past, to present, to future, your sense of responsibility for your own life will be strengthened. Coupled with positive self-influence, a strong sense of responsibility forms a solid foundation on which to anchor that whole life that is yours to live.

• Your past is a rich resource

Your past is history and certainly you cannot go back and live it over again, with new ideas. "The past is gone, forget it" has been oft-repeated advice passed along by well-meaning but ill-advised "philosophers." You can't forget the past, and you shouldn't want to. If you will accept full personal responsibility for your past, including the negative as well as the positive angles, you can make all that history of yours a valuable tool for shaping your future! I repeat, you can convert the past into a dynamic resource for the future, if you will accept the full responsibility for it.

Perhaps you, like many others I have advised, are inclined to be a bit indignant about the suggestion. You feel that you were not responsible for many of the conditions that were forced into your history, especially the negative ones. Well, I agree with you, up to a point. For example, you may have been injured in an accident that was not your fault, or you may have had property stolen from you, or you may have lost your job because your employer gave up the ship. None of them would have been your responsibility. But beyond this type of enforced condition, you were responsible for your *own* action! You may not have consciously accepted the responsibility, and it is that acceptance that I am asking you to consider now. As the value of this acceptance becomes more apparent to you, I know you will say, "I am responsible." So let's display the value.

• Just what has happened in the past?

Facing the past, decide upon a sizable span of time. Make this period about a third of your present birthday total. Thus a person of 40 would consider the immediate past 13 or 14 years of his life. Considering the time span *you* choose, I want you to paint a word picture of everything of consequence that happened to you. This is not going to be too easy to do, and it will have no value as a practical resource if you try to do it as a mental exercise. There is a simple device that will serve most effectively.

Get a piece of paper and a pencil. Place the opened book and the paper in front of you, so that you can use them together. Now, draw a line down the middle of the paper, from top to bottom. At the top, and to the left of the line, write "Negative." On the right of the line write "Positive." Take your pencil and paint that word picture of those past years by making two lists. Letting your memory have free reign, list everything of consequence that happened under either the "negative" heading (as being undesirable, unwanted), or under the "positive" heading (as being desirable, approved).

● **A self-portrait of you**

Take your time, and do a comprehensive job. This is an expansion of that personal inventory you first considered in Chapter 7. Make this a "self-portrait" of your whole life during that period, remembering that every item you list will have value, regardless of which side of the line it is on. Consider the times when problems and complexes were plaguing you and the times when progress and acomplishments were the keynotes. Consider the times when life was confusing and the times when it was inspiring. Consider your health and your experience with self-expression and recognition. Consider your vocational program, your home life and your relations with other people.

When you have finished this review of the past, and you are satisfied that it is a true picture, there will be a number of items in each column.

With your next action, you will take a definite practice step regarding self-influence. Depending upon what you do in this step, you will either influence yourself positively, and face-up to responsibility, or you will influence yourself negatively, and try to compromise with responsibility. Either way you do it, you put a value on the lists. Is there any doubt about the value you want to be on them?

• The "zeros" in your past are important

Now go back over the lists and classify them, item by item. Put a check mark ($\checkmark$) in front of every item that you believe you controlled the influences which made it real in your life. In front of every item that you believe you did not control, because of overpowering outside influences, place a zero (0). If you are in doubt about an item, pass it by for the moment. Eventually you will get them all classified. In fact, I predict that you will go back and change the classification of some, after a bit. You may go back and change some tomorrow, or even next week.

Assuming that you have taken the classification as far as you can at the moment, let's analyze the result. In the negative column you put some check marks. This is a display of commendable fortitude. Where you put zeros in this column, we will assume the decision is justified, but you may also decide to erase some of them later and make them check marks. There are probably more check marks than zeros in the positive column. This is as it should be, because you didn't want a full life then any less than you do now. However, where you did put zeros in this column, you might have been letting undue humility influence you, and you may want to change some to check marks.

• Why your past is recorded as it is

Before you make any changes, and to complete the analysis, let your subconscious memory serve you again. Go back over both lists and mark each item with the reason it carries a check mark or a zero. To save you time, since you would eventually come to this conclusion yourself, let me suggest that one of four terms will describe the reason in each case. These are "planning," "decision," "judgment," and "action" (or "lack of action"). If you will agree with yourself which of the four describes the reason for each check mark or zero, this word picture of you will take on a most remarkable slant. Use your pencil and write the reason after each item.

Now take a look at the lists. The same reasons appear on both the left and right columns. "Decision," for example, appears in the negative column for items marked with zeros and check marks, and it appears in the positive column in the same way. Likewise the other three reasons are indiscriminately scattered through both columns, covering both zeros and check marks. There is great significance in this scattering of the same reasons. It means that there was a definite pattern to your past.

• What you have been responsible for

The pattern shows that "decision" at different times brought about a positive or a negative result, whether there was control by you or outside influence. If, for example, there was a negative outcome induced by an influence you apparently could not control, the real reason it happened was because of your decision to let it happen or because the lack of good judgment allowed it to happen. These reasons, regardless of the source of influence, were your responsibility. Where there was a positive outcome, the real reason it happened was because you started with a plan and acted on that plan. And this, too, was your responsibility.

There is no reason for you to back away from the facts about this responsibility, because this realistic history of your past is providing you with powerful knowledge, knowledge of the picture of your life as a whole, of the whole person that is you. This knowledge is power in your hands, provided you frankly recognize that subconscious self-influence was not enough of a deliberate factor in your past and provided you know where it was, where it was not and why. This you now know.

• Now you know the whys and wherefores

Now you know specifically where negative tendencies shaped your life, and you know what specific self-influence factors to apply to overpower such tendencies in the future. You know where positive tendencies did their good work, and you know that you will increase these tendencies by the deliberate use of more of the same self-influence factors.

So accept the responsibility for the past as being yours, and thus make it an invaluable tool for deliberate self-influence in the future. This acceptance will make a "noteworthy" impression in your subconscious mind. It establishes a positive attitude, one which lays the groundwork for continued responsibility for your own life.

• Any change is your responsibility

You may now want to reconsider some of those zeros on your list. The point is, the more check marks there are on your list, the more realistically you are accepting this responsibility. You know that this is so, because "decision," "planning," "judgment" and "action" all have their source in yourself. You also know that positive subconscious self-influence was a casual, irregular factor in your past. Knowing all of this, you can face responsibility for your future with confidence, because you are perfecting the skill of subconscious self-influence. And you know that it can change your whole life and your whole person.

Don't destroy your "history." We will be referring to it again in the following chapters. Besides, your subconscious has recorded a curiosity about your lists, and it is waiting for you to make the next move in relation to this "first chapter" that you have written.

IN SUM

Examine your past and analyze the influences that shaped it.

This will provide you with a powerful knowledge for more extensive use of self-influence.

15

The Subconscious Mind
and Your Present

WHAT KIND OF A DAY IS THIS FOR YOU? IS IT GOOD, BAD, or indifferent?

If it is "good," you would like to have more like it, because you are enjoying life. If it is "bad," you wish it would get over with. If it is "indifferent," you wish something would happen to change it. You are quite familiar with this variegated pattern of the days, as they come along, aren't you? In fact, this is "life" for you, because life exists only in the present, only in the present moment, only in what you are doing, and feeling, and seeing right now.

What is the secret of why this present moment of "life" is good, bad or indifferent? This "why" should not be a secret, if you want all days to be good days. So let's put the present under a microscope, so to speak, and take a careful look at it.

• Face the present squarely

Turn now, so that you are squarely facing the present. Concentrate on this day, this hour, this moment. Concentrate on your life as it is at this present moment.

You will find that this is a bit difficult to do. It would be difficult for anybody. Even though this is the only time when there is "life" in your history, you find it difficult to concentrate on the present alone. You have already "lived the life" that is in your past, and there is no "life" *yet* in your future. "Life" exists only in the present moment, and this is the most important moment. Yet the "present moment" never seems to possess a distinctiveness all its own. It is always conditioned by what has happened in the past, and by that persistent expectancy for the future.

Much of the time you are consciously aware of this conditioning by the past, and the expectancy of the future. This is the case at this moment, as you concentrate on the present. But, you are subconsciously aware of this "triple-play" reaction 100 per cent of the time. Subconscious activity is constantly proving that the present is directly influenced by the past and that the future is being predicated by the combination of the past and present.

• That will of yours

There is just one factor in your being that is concentrating on the present exclusively. This is that will of yours, sitting at that "control panel" in your conscious mind. This will is directing you to act, react, feel and be what you are at this present moment. Yet you know that this will is constantly influenced by your subconscious and that your subconscious is basing its power on what has already been stored there. Furthermore, because your subconscious is always eagerly anticipating change, and is always ready and willing to help changes come about, your will is influenced by this atmosphere of anticipation. Thus you find it difficult to concentrate on the present alone, because your will is subconsciously influenced by that three-way pull of "past, present and future."

There is a practical, everyday value to this natural function of your subconscious. It is that your whole life and your whole person are constantly being kept in focus, subconsciously. You can take advantage of this by creating a conscious awareness of the whole picture through self-influence. That, in effect, is what you did in the "past history" you wrote in the last chapter. Keeping all these facts in mind, let us create a conscious awareness of the true picture of your present.

• Your past and your present

Put that analysis of the past years in front of you again. Imagine that just off the bottom of the paper, on the table or desk, is a spot that marks the present. Imagine that a separate line is now connecting every separate item in both columns, with that "present" spot. You have a picture of many lines converging at one point. This is a realistic picture of the influence of your "past" on your "present."

This convergence on that spot is symbolic of the constant potential for subconscious influence on what you are doing at any time that is labeled with the "present" in your life. In Chapter 2, you will recall, we defined the four actions that are always affecting your life. These are physical, emotional, intellectual, and spiritual actions. You know that subconscious influence is the major influence that directs your actions in all of these four categories. These four actions add up to create the kind of a "present" you are living. You know that subconscious influence is governed by what has already been stored in your subconscious mind. Therefore these converging lines, from your past to your present, are dramatically indicating two truths. Your whole life, that you are conscious of in this present, has been largely shaped by your past history. And the kind of a person you are, at this present moment, has been largely determined by your actions in the past.

• You can define the effects

Looking objectively at the past history, and considering the lines converging on the present, you can readily define the effects of some of this influence. If there is a negative item on your list that affected your vocational interests, and if you did nothing to overpower it with a positive action, then it has remained on the threshold of your conscious mind ever since. You have the fear that circumstances might repeat themselves and that negative subconscious influence could cause you to have a repeat performance of the negative action. This subconscious negative influence is retarding progressive action in this present time in your life.

Fortunately, positive subconscious influences remain on the threshold of your conscious mind, also. Those positive influences, which are projecting themselves from your past, are looking for an opportunity for repeat performances, too. Your conscious hope is that such opportunities will present themselves.

• The determining balance

What kind of a person you are and what kind of life you have, at this present moment, is determined by the balance between positive and negative subconscious influences, influences that were determined by what you did in the past.

Put simply and directly, you are today what you have done in the past.

But there is one notable exception to much of this, for you. This exception applies to you because of what you have done, and what you are doing, under the guidance of this book of yours. This exception is that you have formulated a plan and you are putting it into practice. This plan gives you control of the subconscious influences that are being recorded today. And this means that you are acquiring the skill of overpowering negative or retarding subconscious influences by deliberate self-influence to create positive influences.

This notable exception means that as you have accepted responsibility for your past, you have also accepted responsibility for your present, and that you have declared to yourself that you are ready, willing and able to accept responsibility for your future, a future with a predetermined pattern to it.

IN SUM

What you are, and how you live your life, is determined by the influences which stem from the past. These influences you are now able to control.

16

The Subconscious Mind
and Your Future

CAN YOU IMAGINE LIFE WITHOUT A FUTURE?

Of course not, because if there were no future, there would be no present!

Think about that for a moment. Much of the tone of the present, and the way you *feel* about the present, is related to the fact that you anticipate a future. If you anticipate the future with enthusiasm, this present moment is a satisfying one. If you anticipate the future with fear, this present moment has a dark cloud hanging over it. But regardless of how you regard the future, you want to have a future.

• You can see the future clearly

But suppose you could control your future and forecast it as "clear and sunny." Would that make a difference in the way you feel and act at this present moment? I know you

144

would answer "Yes!" So let me show you that you can anticipate the future in just that way, with the result that the present moment will be a good one!

Face forward, now, and look into the future!

Looking into the future now, since you have begun this
experience with self-influence, provides a much clearer pre-
view than has been possible in the past. Your future has not
yet been entirely plotted, but parts of it have, and those parts
are clear and distinct. Let's get them into distinct focus. I see
four predetermined elements in your future. Perhaps you can
see more!

• You will control your future

First I see the knowledge that you have acquired through
the progress you have made in your book. This knowledge is
centered on the development of your skill in the use of subconscious self-influence. It has defined your future as something you will control. Certainly the fact that you will apply
this control is clear and distinct, as you look into the future,
now.

The other three clear and distinct elements are the items
listed on your plan that is "in storage" in Chapter 4. Together, these four elements related to your future permit you
to say, "These things I will do. I know what the outcome will
be, and to that extent I know what my future has in store."
But these four are only the beginning. In a few minutes you
will see much more of the future, clearly and distinctly.

Since knowing "why" things happen improves the development of a skill, let's look at "why" these four elements allow
you to see parts of the future so clearly. On the surface, it
would seem that you can see this predetermined action in the
future simply because you have planned to do something
specific. This is a major share of the reason, but it is not the

"whole truth." Recalling those two "keys" to self-control that were given in Chapter 10, we know that there is another significant part to the reason. Those two "keys," as you remember, are the deliberate control of your conscious actions, keeping them on the positive side so that they make a "noteworthy" impression in your subconscious, and the change of negative habit influences by cultivating offsetting positive ones.

• The future will be different

Certainly the four elements we have spotlighted here meet the requirements of the first "key." But what about the second "key"? Are they affecting this clearer picture of the future that you see? They are affecting it, and you can see how by referring to the "history" that you first put together when we discussed your past.

In the last chapter, we projected that "history" and its great influence, into the present. In that intended concept, we realistically pictured the fact that all of the subconscious influences from the past are converging on that one spot marked "the present." We demonstrated that the future is predicted by the combination of the influences of the past and the present. This led us to agree that "you are today what you have done in the past."

• The pattern of your future is in your hands

Now, as though you are holding those facts in one hand, "pick up" the next fact and hold it in the other hand. This fact is that the lines that connected the past with the present, also extend out into the future, indefinitely. Now add this fact. Besides the lines of influence that are extending from your past, you have added some new lines. You have added the four new lines represented by your knowledge of subconscious influence and specific plans.

Now take a look at what you are holding in each hand. In one is the fact that the past predicts the future in your life. In the other is the fact that you have added some new influences today. And remember, tomorrow, today will be "the past." Therefore, instead of the future taking the same old pattern in accordance with the influence of the same old past, it will now be different, in several respects. This means that several negative influences that would have extended the same old way into your future, are being overpowered by some new positive influences. There has been a change in the prediction for the future. This meets the requirement of that second "key." Thus, what you are holding in both hands is evidence the future is predictable.

• Not the same old way of life

Back to that paper that represents the history of the past. Mentally we pictured the lines from each item on your lists converging on the present. Now imagine another spot six inches beyond that spot marking the present. Or imagine it a foot away, or ten feet away. The spot represents the future, the near future, or the future for as long a time ahead as you choose. Before today, before you could look into the future as you are now able to do, you would have had to imagine those lines of influence extending on an unswerving, tedious line, from the present to any spot in the future you imagined. There would be no notable deviation, from present, to near future, to far future. And you, living your life under that influence, would follow that same old path. Probably it is just as well you were not able to see too clearly into the future before today, with that uninspiring prospect ahead of you.

• New paths lead into the future

But today you look into the future and see at least four new and stimulating paths that have been laid out for you. You know that for a part of the time, at least, you are not going to be under the influence of those restrictive negative influences that have been supplied by your subconscious. You know that you have laid the proper groundwork for positive subconscious influences that are stronger than the ragged, time-worn negative ones.

Now, what about time and the pattern of your future? Can goals, objectives or accomplishments be pinned down to specific "times"? Time is a great co-worker with your subconscious. As we have pointed out, your subconscious is always alert, always ready and willing to handle any number of assignments. The passing of time simply means, therefore, that more and more subconscious action is taking place, provided you are stimulating that action, which you are doing.

On the other hand, most of your objectives require that you take progressive steps toward their accomplishment. Some of these steps require physical and intellectual preparation on your part. Most of them require physical and intellectual action, in a step-by-step progressive manner. In other words, little of what you do in the future will happen overnight. You have to use time, physically and mechanically, to reach your objectives.

• Objectives are important

Your subconscious mind is geared to go along with these time requirements. But more than that, you can let your subconscious set the pace by which you will use time. While your subconscious is reminding you of your objectives, and encouraging you to keep moving toward them, it will also recognize deadlines, provided you consciously set them up along with your plans.

Consider the items that are in your Chapter 4 plans. Let's say that you added deadlines to the plans. (Deadlines are highly recommended! More about them later.) Suppose you said that you would accomplish one of them in two days, one within a week and the other in ten days. This is assuming that each is physically and mechanically possible within those periods. You add these deadlines to your plans so that they, too, make a "noteworthy" impression on your subconscious. There won't be the slightest conflict in your subconscious because of these three different time factors. The result? As each of those deadlines appear on the calendar, you will find yourself checking off the predicted item as "mission accomplished!" In this way you can peg down at least three specific times in your future when a predetermined accomplishment will be met.

• Your dreams can come true

I never recommend that people go in for daydreaming. I don't think that anyone can afford it. But I do recommend that people, at times, let themselves deliberately "dream" a bit, especially when such "dreaming" will permit a stimulating panorama of the future to appear before them. Such dreaming is good for you because it lets you take a big look at things, and taking a big look often whets the appetite for *doing* more to *make* more dreams come true. I suggest that you "dream" a bit right now.

Remember those fifteen items in Chapter 4, the fifteen from which you chose three for your initial plans? Perhaps you should turn back to that chapter for a minute and glance over those fifteen items, to get a picture of the scope of life they represent.

Now, "dreaming" a bit, picture what your life would be like

today if all fifteen were planned as actions in your life for the future! Picture what the future would be like! Picture having a long succession of "accomplishment days" appear on the calendar!

A pleasant "dream"? Yes, for the moment. But not for long! What you are "dreaming" about now represents a lot of things you will have to do something about, if you want them to come true. But they are all things that you can do, so now stop dreaming. Read Chapter 17: the title there is, "You and Your Subconscious Mind as Partners in Action." Here is your future!

IN SUM

Your future is predictable.
You, and only you, can make it so.
You can help yourself by setting "deadlines" for the completion of your plans for the future.

• • •

SUMMARY OF PART TWO
YOUR PRACTICE

• You have been objective in evaluating yourself.

• You now know, therefore, what changes in your life you want to make.

• In this task, you have a powerful partner—your subconscious.

- This partner has recorded your life's experiences, your past. Accept responsibility for the past and make it a tool.

- You now know the keys of self-influence: one the controlling of conscious actions to make them noteworthy and the other the substituting of positive habits for negative ones.

- You also know that the secret of subconscious power lies in deliberate preparation and a conscious predetermination of the outcome.

- You must want the best results from your activity.

- Your future is predictable, but only by you, and through your actions.

- Set deadlines for the successful completion of your actions. They are all practice steps in acquiring self-influence.

- Meet those deadlines.

- When you have done this, you are ready for the next step—perfecting your new power.

● ● ●

PART THREE

PERFECTION

You and Your Subconscious Mind as Partners in Action

Your Subconscious Power—How to Make It Work for You is the title of your book, and now you are ready for a direct application to your life.

Is this a "magic power" you are dealing with? Yes, it is. When its demonstrated effects are considered, it can be seen that your subconscious produces results as if by some "magic power." "Magic" is usually associated with "mysteriousness" and to many persons, the action of the subconscious is mysterious. No longer is this so for you, since we have removed the mystery. In a sense, you are becoming a "magician" in relation to your subconscious. A magician "makes magic" only after much preparation and after carefully setting the stage. Preparation and stage setting are also requirements for use of the power of your subconscious, as you have learned.

• Stop daydreaming

You are going to "make magic" through subconscious self-influence. What's more, you are never going to get over the feeling of wonderment at the apparently "magic" results of such self-influence. I am sure that there isn't a person, including you, who has not done some daydreaming about a wonderful life that *could* be, if only some magic wand would put a magic power at his disposal. The point is you don't have to daydream any longer, because a "magic power" has been put at your disposal.

• The "magic power" is within you

However, as you now very well know, the effective use of this magic power depends upon your subconscious mind being in action, positive, controlled action. The magic power we are talking about is not in this book, *per se*, but it is in you, and in the application of the principles of subconscious self-influence in your life. The secret of using this power lies in a dynamic partnership, the partnership of you and your subconscious mind in action. That, too, you already know. Your book, up to this point, has been a tool for planning, for preparation, and for acquiring knowledge. It has now totally served that purpose. At this point your book becomes a tool for practice, and it will take a moment or two to convert the book to this new use.

First, remove that list that has been serving as a bookmark at Chapter 4. Keep it handy, however. It's now a practice tool. You also need three other pieces of paper or cards that can serve as new bookmarks. You are going to put an identifying title at the top of each so that the titles can be seen when the bookmarks are put in place. At the top of one bookmark, write the words "Practice Projects." On another, write "Creed" and on the third, write "The 3 rules." Place the first at the beginning of Chapter 4. Place the second at Chapter 11 and the third at Chapter 13. The purpose of this is to provide finger-tip reference points, to which you will often refer in the practice steps. With the addition of a pencil and note paper at hand, your book is now a tool for the "partners" to use.

- **You have made yourself ready**

Take a moment to re-establish a strong, conscious awareness of the significance of those three bookmarks. Being consciously aware of what is at your fingertips in those three marked chapters puts you on the "ready line" for action. You are already quite familiar with Chapter 4. That was the source of your "practice projects." But re-read the title there: "Self-Influence Is the Key to the Pattern of Your Life." That's another reason why the bookmark is placed there.

The title of Chapter 11, where the second bookmark is placed, is "The New Positive Concept of Self-Control." Here's where your "creed" is stated, of course. Do you still have a pretty good picture of that statement of action? It might be a good idea to quickly re-read it. Obviously, Chapter 13, which is also bookmarked, contains those "three rules" for turning on the power of your subconscious, as the chapter title states. Paraphrasing the chapter titles we get a statement that indicates the strong action that is inherent in the contents. These are: "Self-influence, positive concept, use the power!" All ready? Step forward, then!

- **You have tested that power**

Action started with the list of three projects and action continues with the same list. This list is right in front of you now, but you hardly need to refer to it now, do you? Sometime back, you put your subconscious power to work on the list; you no longer need this mechanical aid to remind you of your specific plans. Let's see if what you did in relation to these plans met the requirements of the three rules. Checking at the book-marked spot, we recall the rules called for (1) deliberate conditioning of your subconscious; (2) wholeheartedly wanting to follow through; (3) letting the power of your subconscious work with you. You did follow those rules, in relation to your plans, and they did work, didn't they?

Now, "all ears," please! The same process, based on the same rules, and interpreted by you in the same way, will put those plans into action and bring them to the point of accomplishment!

There are three stepping-stones to accomplishment, with your subconscious as your partner. These stepping-stones put the word "plan" in the background (but most certainly do not eliminate the word). Now you have superimposed the word "goals" over the subjects on the paper. The three stepping-stone goals are (1) The major goal (which is what you said you would do, in your plans); (2) The deadline goal (which defines when things will happen); and (3) The step-by-step goals (which define how things will happen).

• Goals are all-important

Each one of these steps is an element of positive action. All three are required to support your "do, positively" creed. (Check back and confirm this!) The major goal is necessary, because it defines the accomplishment you are after and sets it up as a "bright star" in your future. The deadline goal is necessary because it puts time into a favorable progressive relationship with your goal. You must say "when," or you are, in effect, saying "never." The step-by-step goals are necessary because all accomplishment is dependent upon taking the first step, then the second, and so forth. This is the practical viewpoint of the person with accomplishment in his spirit. Furthermore, you will find that "step-by-step" things go smoothly and easily, and that each step is a form of accomplishment. Leave out the "how" goal, and you jeopardize your membership in the "no mystery to life" club. There is no mystery to step-by-step accomplishment!

Now, how do these stepping-stones of action hold up in the face of your "do" creed? Check back and you'll see that the creed is based upon performance, production, accomplishment, saying "do" rather than talking about it, or wishing, or waiting. The action-goal approach holds up beautifully to these requirements, doesn't it?

• Your subconscious in action

Now to bring your subconscious into full partnership with you, in action. Action is to be related to the three practice projects you chose from Chapter 4. For your own sake, please don't deviate from that basic plan of action. You are in an enviable position in relation to your future, because of the self-preparation you have made so far, with these specific projects. Many, many people would "give anything" to be in your position, if they only knew how. Action here is a prologue to extended action that will soon come, and that will encompass all of your life. So, stick to those specific projects. Besides, by doing so, you find that you have already reached the first stepping-stone, the establishment of your major goal in each instance.

• First step forward

So, consciously you have already made a noteworthy impression on your subconscious, and three major goals have been established. Thus you have reached the first stepping-stone in action, with your subconscious in partnership. Are those goals really "bright stars" in your future? Most certainly they are, so let's go to work and get them! There is note paper and a pencil in front of you. Put on paper when you will "get" those stars, and reach those major objectives. Make a truly noteworthy recording in your subconscious by putting accomplishment dates alongside your major goals. You know that they will make noteworthy impressions on your subconscious, because a deadline on accomplishment is an unusual, abnormal occurrence in anybody's life! So now you have impressionably recorded three deadline goals! That's stepping-stone number two.

How will you act in each case? To answer that, let's come to real frank terms about ourselves. There has never been a time when either of us really wanted to do something and wanted the results to pay off quickly, that we didn't know how to do it. For every goal and objective, big or small, that I have established in my life, I have always known how to reach it. This has been almost a natural consequence of setting a goal, and quite logically so. Every objective was put in the spotlight in my life in answer to a basic human urge. Subconsciously I had stored away knowledge and observations of the experiences of others and subconsciously there was a "file," built by interest in the objective, which told me that I could do this something, if I wanted to. But also with every objective, there has been the need to take the first step, and then the second . . . and so on. Logically then, I have always known that I could reach an objective, provided I subconsciously supported that step-by-step action.

• Then, many steps forward

This has been true about every person who has been related to my classes or courses; and like us, it is true about you. You really know what to do to accomplish each of the three goals we are concerned with here. Now, bring your subconscious in action into partnership by letting it work with you, step by step. Right now, consciously make an impression on your subconscious and turn that power on, by picking up your pencil and listing the step-by-step action you will take to meet that deadline for each goal!

Now let's take a look at where you stand. You have three major goals prominently established in your life. You have predetermined their accomplishment with realistic deadlines. You have plotted the steps you will take, starting with the first one in each case.

• Nothing can stop you

You can prove to yourself that your subconscious power is ready to back up action—and prove that you are consciously and subconsciously primed for action—through a simple experiment. Make another visual and mental review of these action steps and your goals. Then go on about your normal business. Pick up the routine of work, play, travel, or whatever. You will find that you have a persistent urge to take those first steps, regardless of what else you are doing. You won't be able to forget the pending action. In fact, you will be impelled by a drive to "get going." This will be so because your subconscious power is pushing you, urging you to act. All you have to do is let it push you and you will find yourself easily and smoothly in action on the first steps toward all three goals.

Now you are in action, deliberately planned and controlled action, positive action! This action was conceived by subconscious self-influence. It will continue under the same influence. You are now consciously acting in accordance with this self-induced influence. This is so because your subconscious is your partner in action. And this is a practice step that is the first step in establishing a positive habit of action that will expand to affect your everyday life.

But right now, isn't this the status in life that you have long considered ideal?

IN SUM

It is time for action.
You are ready to do, positively.
There are three stepping stones:
Defining your major goal;
Setting a deadline; and
Step-by-step action.

---

o→ RESULT-GETTING PROJECTS ←o

Since this is a first comprehensive experience for you in the control of action through subconscious self-influence, let me make a suggestion to you that can serve to bolster up this first major practice step. I suggest that you remember that you have all of those pertinent resources at hand, in the preceding chapters of your book; and I suggest that you use the resources to help make this a bell-ringing experience for yourself.

Re-read Chapter 4, if you need to confirm why you are doing all this. Check through Chapter 2, to prove the value of participation, which you are now called upon to do, with 100 per cent of your will. Re-read Chapter 5 to see why this is taking the "mystery" out of life for you. See how this action fits that best model in humans, as described in Chapter 6. Re-read Chapter 10, and see how you have created an ideal condition in your subconscious. Compare your present status with the analysis you made of your past in Chapter 14, and see what a difference there now is in this action. Take advantage of the suggestions made in Chapter 11, in bringing subconscious power into play all the way.

In other words, you are bringing your subconscious into positive partnership through action. Be sure that it is perfect action!

18

You and Your Subconscious Mind
as Partners in Action
... in Your Everyday Life

How did you start this day? Did you get up saying, "oh boy, do I feel good!"

Did you look out the window, at the world, and say, "Things look pretty fine out there!"

While you were eating breakfast, did you have the feeling that you were anxious to get going and get things done, good things, that is?

If you did not start the day this way, why didn't you? There is no valid reason not starting every day this way, and if you are being truthful with yourself, you know that. In fact, I believe you did start the day feeling good about everybody and everything, including yourself. I believe this because it is the natural outcome of the experiences you are having in self-influence.

164

• It's a wonderful feeling!

It's wonderful to feel that you are on the side of "good fortune" in life, such as you are feeling, now that you have taken the first steps toward those goals. Surpassing a *similar* feeling you had in the past, this one is superior because you brought it about by yourself. Even more important is the fact that the "die is cast" and that you have established a foothold on a bright future by the effective practice of the skill of self-influence. By intensifying this influence in your everyday life, the "life is good" feeling will not be an unusual or uncommon feeling. It will be an everyday feeling.

It has always been a stimulating experience for me to see the people I have worked with arrive at this point. I have seen people with habit—ingrained fears get full release from their apprehensions and qualms through their first experiences with positive self-control. I have seen others who were "puppets" of circumstance cast off the strings of negative influence and begin to act on their own initiative, like mature adults, after similar demonstrations of subconscious self-influence. In fact, do you remember those first five "models" of human beings described in Chapter 7? I have seen real-life replicas of all of them go through an experience similar to yours and have had them tell me, "I didn't know life could be so different, so easily!" That is how I know that in some way you are experiencing an unusual experience about the "goodness of life," right now.

• There is much more ahead

However, as fine as the situation was, it was not where I stopped working with those people. Nor is this the place for you and me to part company. Certainly those people had established a positive attitude toward self-control, just as you have. But the major goal with them, as with you, is to convert that attitude into a habit. The experience you have had with the three projects is really but the first step toward that major goal. So, keep in step with me, and your book, and take more of those action steps.

Obviously we are going to be concerned about positive self-influence in your everyday life. But I want to caution you that I am talking about a different kind of everyday life than has been "everyday" for you in the past. I warned you that this was coming when I predicted that yours would be an "abnormal" life, remember? But I know that this is the way you want it. The next steps are based on the concept of life we discussed in Chapter 5. Quoting from that chapter: "What else is there in life except to *have* beliefs, to *act* progressively and to *get along* with others?" (The answer is, of course: that's the ideal that anybody would want!) Again quoting: "An everyday diet of that kind of living is almost ideal, isn't it?" We can only answer "Yes."

• What has been good is good today

With that ideal life in view, we are coming close to the climax point in the practice steps. We began preparing for this climax back in Chapter 1. Remember those "agreements" you made with yourself in Chapter 2 and the demonstrations that you made? They were related to belief, progressive action and getting along with others. What better way to "get along" with another person than to render him a service? Now consider the three practice projects you chose from Chapter 4. When you got into action on those, you found that each was related to the three parts of an "ideal life." Is it not logical, therefore, to consider them a continuation and expansion of such self-controlled action as would result in an ideal everyday life? Of course it is, so let's get to work on that goal.

The answers to how to do it are at your fingertips, at those bookmarked spots in your book. We will start at that spot marked "Practice steps" . . . Chapter 4. There are, of course, fifteen projects listed there, of which you have used three. Our objective here is get the remaining dozen into action. We will do this in accordance with your bookmarked "Creed" and bookmarked "Three rules."

• Practical needs are important

First, let's see why the practice projects are classified into three groups. This is done because the groups represent the three most important areas of influence in your life. The first group, which includes time, money, energy, health and the future, is concerned with the most significant "practical" influences in your life. The degree to which these factors are substantial in your life makes the "practical" side of living have plus or minus values.

• The bright side is important

The second group, which includes love, contentment, peace of mind, adventure, and "looking your best," is concerned with factors that produce an inner glow, bring warmth into your life. The degree to which these factors are "alive" or "dead," determines whether you feel that all's well with the world.

• Self-importance is important

The third group, which includes achievement, recognition, self-expression, personality, and happiness, is concerned with factors that establish your personal integrity and support your importance to yourself. The degree to which these are obvious or subdued in your life determines how well you are meeting your purpose in life.

When you selected those first practice steps, you practiced conscious and subconscious self-control over a "practical" influence, a warming "inner glow" influence, an influence related to your personal integrity. When you went into action on these projects, you supported that ideal concept of life based upon beliefs, progressive action and good relationships. You can and will establish an "everyday" relationship with this concept by putting the rest of the projects into action all together and at the same time!

• Load up your subconscious!

"All together, and at the same time?" Yes, by turning on all the power of your subconscious! Your subconscious is willing and able to handle this load. Your conscious will and your conscious intellect and emotions also have the capacity for handling this load. All of this is so because the "load" represents the everyday life of the kind of a person you are modeling yourself to be! That "ideal" life for that "ideal" person is full of action, and the capacity for this action can now be substantiated in your life, through more subconscious self-influence.

In taking this next step, you are going to become more aware of the phenomena of your subconscious that were demonstrated in the first three practice steps. You "felt good" about the resultant experiences because your subconscious was doing more work for you than you realized. Because you used positive self-influence, and acted accordingly, you energized your subconscious to put out more "power" than came from the effect of immediate conscious influence. About each of those projects you said, in effect: "This is good! I can do it. I will do it." And you acted. Immediately your subconscious searched through those "files" of past experience and memory and brought to light many positive items that had been stored away there, unused. Your subconscious "matched up" many other "good" items that had been previously placed there with the positive "good" action you had brought about through self-influence. This "matching up" process is a *bonus* of power that your subconscious supplies after you first turn on the power, through self-influenced action. This phenomena will be a factor in the next twelve practice steps. In fact, what you have already done through the first three steps, will also be used by your subconscious to add more power to other projects in the future. That's the kind of a partner to have, isn't it? It is willing to work overtime to make you "feel good" about life every day, if you will just give it a chance and let it work!

• A red letter day for you

I don't have to tell you what to do now, do I? The fact that a "red letter day" is at hand for you is now more than obvious. I have the same vision of that day as you do, and it is wonderful! I am picturing you confidently setting about to make it happen. I see you with a bigger sheet of paper in front of you that will enable you to list twelve practice projects, as compared to the three listed on that first important piece of paper. I see you turning to Chapter 4 and listing the project titles, and answering all the questions. I see you putting a deadline date after each project. Finally, I see you having a stimulating experience putting down the step-by-step accomplishment procedure. When you have finished, I can hear you saying to yourself: "I am going to be a busy person!" And that you are, busy about an everyday life that is "the best."

At this point I can see you doing something else. You recall that "imaginary" retreat that was your experience in Chapter 8 and you are establishing yourself in a similar atmosphere gain. In this session with yourself and BY yourself, I visualize you taking your time to influence yourself with the contents of those other two bookmarked chapters, Number 11, your creed, and Number 13, the three rules. You are thoughtfully relating the contents of those chapters to your expanded list of practice projects. Here, neither you nor I can "see" what else is happening, but we know that through this "retreat" action you are causing the power of subconscious self-influence to be directly related to the projects.

• Action and accomplishment are "twins"

This is the point where the subconscious power is turned on and you feel that urge to act. I can see you take the first steps toward many accomplishments. All of this is the way you "see" yourself acting, isn't it? I have no doubt about it because I know that you have no doubts about yourself!

For the moment, we are going to "jump ahead" a bit, and project a bit of predetermined action related to your immediate future. We have talked about habit, the habit of positive self-influence. Any possibility for a consistent pattern of everyday life such as we have plotted here is incontestably related to subconscious self-influence. Subconscious self-influence will best become a habit by deliberate repetition of influence on your conscious will, such as you are doing in putting all of the practice steps into action. Therefore, if we project a time in your immediate future while you are in the process of taking those "in between steps," we can see the establishment of the habit of subconscious self-influence. So, while *these* practice steps are bringing about immediate tangible results, they are also establishing a tendency on your part to subconsciously repeat the action.

• Opportunities unlimited

You are now in prime condition to accept all the many new opportunities for positive self-influence. Once you have reached this point, which is just ahead for you, the pattern of your everyday life under this new concept will be constantly maintained and every day will be a "red letter day!"

In that "retreat" that prepared you for the pattern of expanded positive action, I am sure you found that some deadline dates had to be placed a bit further ahead than others, because the first action steps require you to do a bit more preparation or to bolster up your knowledge or skill in a particular area. That was the realistic thing to do, and even though you may not move as fast with those projects, at first, you did put yourself into action!

• Self-influence will grow and prosper

Just ahead are a series of chapters that are provided to meet such needs for a bit more knowledge and skill. These chapters cover areas of life where other persons, like yourself, have felt the greatest need for a "helping hand." All of the subjects are important to you but some will have greater significance than others. They will help you to round out the pattern of a wonderful every day life. Use them as additional tools for subconscious self-influence.

Now, fifteen practice projects in positive self-influence in action! This does give you the status of a very busy person, and a most important person. So I will leave you while you get at it. When we "meet" again, a bit later in your book, I will be meeting the new model you, the more important you. Until then, "more power" to you!

IN SUM

The positive attitude you now have toward self-influence must be converted into a habit.

This you can do through practice, i.e., through deliberate repetition of influence on your conscious will.

Remember, the "load" on your subconscious can never be too great, because the "ideal" life for an "ideal" person is full of action.

19

You and Your Subconscious Mind as Partners in Action
. . . in Relation to Faith

FROM A COLLECTION OF EPITAPHS PUBLISHED BY SOME whimsical person, I have always remembered this one:

> Here lies dead Jim Horner,
>   Life's end for him was grim;
> He put faith in fate,
>   But fate put no faith in him.

That is a bit of a tongue-twister, but it really says something very true about the lives of many persons. I don't know anything about Jim. Perhaps he put too much faith in his ability to draw a gun first. Nor do I know anything about the author of that bit of verse. But certainly he was an observant, practical philosopher. I feel that he wasn't concerned with simply supplying an epitaph for Jim; he knew that others would read the

173

message, and perhaps he was suggesting that this fellow's brush with fate could be an object lesson for others.

As I said, I think that this macabre "poet" knew what he was talking about, except that his horse-sense observation was a bit late to do Jim any good. Many, many people walk around wearing a "living" epitaph like that one. Over the years and by the hundreds, I've seen them as members of my classes and home study courses, and this "epitaph" had to be removed before they could go on living a life of true faith.

• Blind faith is misleading

I should like to change that verse a bit, to fit the living. Trying my hand at very free verse, I would put it this way:

> There goes a certain good person,
> To whom fortune is but a wraith;
> He puts blind faith into his fate,
> But his fate doesn't match his faith.

Too many people blindfold themselves by their interpretation of faith. To them faith is a passive condition, with the outcome in the hands of fate, which guides them along unpredictable paths. Actually both faith and fate are "mysteries" to these people.

Then there are others who blindfold themselves by denying the value of faith in their lives. They try to wrestle with fate, single-handedly, apparently believing that a "practical, matter-of-fact" attitude gives them an upper hand.

That "living epitaph" fits both kinds of people, unfortunately so. As you now know, no one is supposed to go through life blindfolded . . . and no one can be blindfolded about faith and live a full life.

• True faith opens all doors

However, there is that legion of people to whom faith is like an all-seeing eye in their lives, opening doors to a radiant interpretation of a full life. I am inclined to try my hand again at a verse describing that kind of a person, only this is not an epitaph, but rather the rule of a "blue ribbon" winner in life. About this kind of a person I would say:

> Now here is a right-living person,
>   For whom things in life are just great;
> He puts his faith into action,
>   And works hand-in-hand with his fate!

Whether you have been branded with that "living epitaph" or not, I encourage you to adopt this rule about faith because it fits hand-in-glove with your new creed of life and with the three rules.

Faith and fate should be combined in a positive partnership in your life. Action is the key to that partnership, action induced by that ever-active partner of yours, the power of your subconscious.

• Faith is belief in action

Faith is not intended to be a passive condition. True faith is an energized condition, based upon demonstrations of belief, of trust, of reliance. Nor is fate unconditionally an enigma, bringing a person face to face with unheralded circumstances. There is a power in your life that foreordains your lot in life, but it can be made a productive power because it is subject to your influence. But an energized faith and an influenced fate require responsibilities of the person who wants them related to his life. He cannot approach the one "blindly," nor the other "inevitably." He must keep his eyes open, and know what he is doing and know why!

> ". . . He puts his faith into action,
> And works hand-in-hand with his fate!"

How? By capitalizing on the experience of others who have proved the substantiality of faith, by demonstrating faith and by acting according to his distinctiveness as his Creator would have him act. All of this you can do through positive self-influence, backed by the power of your subconscious.

One definition of faith is: "believing without proof." I believe that this is an illogical definition. Belief by an individual is based upon trust and reliance upon something held to be true. Isn't that your interpretation of belief? If you hold something to be true, you must have had some proof of its authenticity. I hold that every circumstance worthy of your faith can offer proof of its right to be believed in and that, if you seek the truth, you will find the proof and the basis of your faith.

• Faith in your god

Let us wade right into that most common application of faith, religious faith, and apply that premise here. An abridged definition of religion is that it is an earthly plan of recognition of a Supreme Being and the worship of Him as the ultimate Father of mankind. Now, if there were no churches, per se, in the world, would people have a "plan" of recognition of a Supreme Being? I believe that we would have such a plan, because man is a reasoning animal, and there is so much proof in the world of a supernatural Intelligence. Consider some of this proof.

"Man cannot make man, only God can make a man." True

or false? True! Even though man and woman are the necessary partners in the conception and birth of a child, they do not "give life" to the union of cells, nor can they endow the child with its basic intelligence, nor infuse it with the spirit that makes it a human being. As physical agents in a birth, they must rely on life, and intelligence and spirit coming to the child from "somewhere else" or from "someone else." Is it not true, therefore, that this "something" exists, since its manifestation is so constant?

• Man is related to a creative plan

"Man is a self-sufficient animal." True or false? False! As definite as we are in asserting in this book of yours that you *can* shape your life, we do so only because we can rely upon a basic plan that is beyond our influence. A common name for this plan is "Nature." This includes the natural creativeness of the world itself, the acts of growth and replenishment. You could have no "plan of life" if it were not for the productive earth, the seasons, the cycle of the sun. Consistency in that plan makes consistency possible in your plan, and, yet, the former is in no sense man-made. We cannot conceive of such consistency without the existence of some kind of a governing intelligence. We know we are not entirely self-sufficient. We have faith in the Supreme Intelligence that provides Nature's plan.

• Man's faith in man

Besides birth and nature, another proof of the existence of a Supreme Being lies in the inherent "brotherhood" of man. No, I am not being irrational. You and I have already agreed that "man" often abuses or disavows this "brotherhood" concept, but you now know how to establish your relationship to such conditions. You possess the basic urges that demand satisfaction in life. So does everyone else. These urges can only be satisfied through companionship with others, in one form or another. The desire for companionship is inborn. To the extent that everyone was "made alike," has found his greatest prosperity and accomplishment through community living. This desire is not man-made. It is given to him because he needs it. Here is another proof of some guiding Intelligence. And to that extent, we put faith in His "brotherhood" plan every day of our lives.

Obviously man has found that faith in the Supreme Being is fostered by corporate effort. The many churches and doctrines in the world are unions of people who believe in a Supreme Plan. The words and methods of such plans vary, but I know of no religious union that asks anyone to accept a faith "blindly." Every person is encouraged to seek "proof" as an individual, and he is encouraged to demonstrate his faith and to live his faith. Every person who has done this has "felt" the partnership of his God in his life, but it first required action on his part.

Therein lies the value of any object of faith in your life. Every bit of evidence of the value and power of faith indicates that it must be a deep-rooted condition, with the "roots" in the subconscious mind. To be of real value in your life, faith must be an influence that is always on tap. The only means you have of creating an ever-present inner influence is through the conditioning of your subconscious. And, of course, you *now* know that deliberate action is the key to positive subconscious influence.

• Keep faith with yourself

You have already laid the foundation for dynamic faith in your life, through your first efforts in the practice steps. Primarily, you have demonstrated faith in yourself, and faith in the future. You did this by deliberate planned action. From now on, faith in yourself and the future will grow in value and power, because your subconscious will remind you of the proved realness of faith in these actions. You can go on proving it, for all of your days. You did not go about it "blindly," and it was not "blind faith." And certainly you did not disavow its potential power by harboring doubt about the outcome.

• Faith induces optimism

There is great significance in this phase of faith in your life. Faith is really the basic ingredient in the preparatory steps in any positive action. Faith establishes an influence that is based upon optimism and the anticipation of positive outcomes. It establishes a basic belief in an action. Frankly, this influence of dynamic faith is at the core of the predetermination of good outcomes. And therein lies establishment of the right relationship with fate. If fate is to be considered a predetermined definition of your lot in life, then through this practice of dynamic faith, you are working hand-in-hand with your fate.

Where, then, in your life is the establishment of dynamic faith needed, and thereby a good working relationship with faith? You have already established it in relation to yourself, and to your immediate future. What about the future a year from now, ten years from now? What about your God? What about other people, with whom you live, or work, or play? What about your marriage partner, your family, your children? What about your country, and democracy? What about that important matter of health, and the enjoyment of life? And what about "rightness," and your belief in your basic purpose in life? Do you need to establish or strengthen your faith in any of these factors in your life? If you do, do it! Do it by making your faith dynamic. Do this by applying your creed of "do, positively" and through the use of the "three rules."

• Make faith a basic influence

Define every thing you want to believe in, everything and everybody in which you have the need or desire for perfection. Define where you need to establish faith in any relationship and where you need to strengthen it. Say: "These are the things in which I want to have faith. Then make the faith dynamic by applying subconscious self-influence.

I vividly remember a husband and wife, participants in one of my home study courses, who came face to face with the fact that faith had been a misunderstood, passive factor in their lives. They said that they believed in most of the desirable things that other good people did. Yet most of the "proof" that appeared to manifest itself in their lives was negative proof, until it seemed that their faith was all wrong. The well-educated husband had never risen above the subordinate level in his work. The conscientious wife had never achieved a feeling of fulfillment. They were quite willing to say that, despite their faith, fate was against them.

When, through the searching personal analysis that is part of the course, we showed them that they had been just sitting back hoping that faith would work for them, they took "deep breaths" and made some active demonstrations of their faith. From then on, they were living in a different world. Both husband and wife have found fulfillment since then, through living their faith.

• Dynamic faith for you

Briefly, then, faith must be dynamic to have any value in your life. Determine where your beliefs that are dependent on faith must be centered. Deliberately go into action in support of those beliefs, and put your subconscious power to work on them. Bring dynamic faith into your life in order to put fate on your side. Brand yourself with that rule of the person who interprets life radiantly. Make that rule read:

> "Here am I, a right-living person,
>   For whom things in life are just great;
> I have put my faith into action,
>   And work hand-in-hand with my fate!"

IN SUM

In preparing for positive action, faith is the basic ingredient.

Strengthen your faith. Make it dynamic.

This you will do through action and, thus, through your subconscious and self-influence.

o→ RESULT-GETTING PROJECTS ←o

Everything that you have done so far in your experience with positive self-influence has prepared the way for dynamic faith in your life. Your move is to put "belief in action" into your life. Get into action through these projects.

1. Eliminate doubt as a factor of fear, or mistrust, skepticism or insincerity. Where any of these elements of doubt exist in your life, put them under the spotlight of truth. You can have faith in nothing and nobody when doubt is a factor. Like a crusader, seek the facts about

any situation or any relationship. Seek until you find the genuineness that is there, the elements of integrity. If, in any case, you find that these elements are not there, you know that faith would be misplaced, and that removes doubt. Most often you will find the core of integrity, that is true. Concentrate your understanding on the positive element that you can believe in and act upon! Eliminate doubt by seeking the truth!

2. Establish an attitude of optimism in the things and people in which and in whom you are placing your faith. Optimism acts like a great "preservative" of faith. It will keep your faith alive in the face of assaults by negative "outside influences." Optimism is a subconscious influence that puts the brightest coloring on faith. Maintain optimism by keeping the truth in constant focus and your subconscious will prompt you to put your beliefs into action at the proper time.

3. *Let* faith be a dynamic factor by anticipating good outcomes as you put your beliefs into action. Are you concerned about fate in your life? Then have faith in your fate by anticipating your fate positively! As optimism puts the right "coloring" on your faith, anticipation puts "flavor" into it. It puts life into your faith, because you anticipate nothing but the best from your "beliefs in action."

> Eliminate doubt; replace it with truth.
> Be optimistic about the truth.
> Anticipate positive outcomes from your dynamic faith.

Plot the application of faith this way, and subconscious self-influence will make it real in relation to your creator, your future, your family life, your purpose in life and in all relationships with people and conditions.

20

You and Your Subconscious Mind as Partners in Action ...in Relation to Knowledge and Learning

THE PERSON WHO KNOWS WHAT TO DO KNOWS ALL THERE is to know!

The person who knows when to do "what" has learned to use knowledge properly!

The person who knows what to do, and when to do it, is in a position to control most of the influences in his life!

The person who uses knowledge and learning as the basis for a self-influenced life is using the power of his subconscious mind to the fullest extent!

In those four statements is a concept of knowledge and learning that perfectly fits the concept of that promised "new life" for you.

Most people would agree that knowing "what to do, at the right time" would be a pretty convenient skill for anyone to have. They would say that such a person would be a "smart one," and they would say it enviously. Secretly, everybody wishes to possess this skill. The lack of it causes many persons to withdraw in fear of "doing the wrong thing at the wrong time." Actually anybody can acquire this skill, because it is all based upon knowledge and learning, and knowledge is one of the "freest" things in the world, backed by opportunities for learning that have no limit.

• Strengthen your life through learning

There is much more to all this than being "convenient" to know what to do, and when. Most important to you is the fact that this concept puts you in a stronger position to control influences, and the fact that knowledge and learning is good "red meat" that your subconscious thrives on! Even beyond that is the bonus I hinted at when I said that you "know all there is to know" when you know what to do! This is a positive statement that you are ready to accept, aren't you? Because life is action, and doing, and if you know what to do, what else is there to know? As the result of the conditioning of your subconscious, it will prompt you as to when, at the right time.

Let's run a test on this theory. We will put two recurring conditions to the test, conditions that have affected everyday living for you, and which could well be factors right now. Because these conditions are at opposite ends of the scale in emotional as well as practical effects, you will be able to judge whether this theory has universal or limited application.

We will consider "problems" and "opportunities," and the relation of knowledge to these recurring factors in life. You can make this a *personal* test by considering a problem of your own, and an opportunity that is yours, at this time. *Both* are influences in your life arising mostly from "outside forces." These influences *differ* in that the problem is a negative influence and the opportunity a positive one. But they are *alike* in that both call for action. As simple as it may sound, the fact is that if you know what to do, in both cases, you could act properly. *Unless you act*, the problem can grow to out-of-bounds proportions, and, *unless you act*, the opportunity can wither and die on the vine. Knowledge of "what to do" is necessary to control both this positive and this negative influence. And of course *you know* that if you don't initiate controlled action, these influences will *cause* uncontrolled action in your life, in spite of your "wishes."

• Knowledge conquers problems

Let's put the "problem" through the mill first. There are two well-stocked sources of knowledge to draw from. The first is conscious observation. This means to deliberately consider every fact about the problem and your relationship to it. Every problem does more than just "exist." Something caused it, and that "something" is the true core of the problem. Every problem causes a lot of "ifs" to sprout. "If I had done differently, if 'that' had happened instead of 'this,' if I could only do 'that' now." These are some of the "ifs" that have plagued you. But none of them is really the problem. When you want to put out a fire, you attack the flame, not the smoke. Those "ifs" are just smoke. So, first identify the single, elemental fact of the problem and concentrate on that. This is workable knowledge!

• There is just one right answer

Second, just as deliberately, determine what you can and should do to cancel out that problem. Consider the best answer, not the second best or any kind of a compromise, and concentrate on that. This is the knowledge of "what to do" that you need. Up to this point, then, you have defined the single truth of what the problem is, and you have defined the best action. Now we might say that all you have to do is take a deep breath, "get up the nerve," and go ahead and lick the problem. That could work, but you would be making it unnecessarily rough on yourself because you have another source of knowledge to draw upon that will strengthen your action a hundred per cent. This is the power of your subconscious mind.

Assign the knowledge you have consciously learned to your subconscious. Assign your intention to act to your subconscious. These impressionable assignments will bring your subconscious into action and cause it to reveal other serviceable knowledge and experience that has been stored subconsciously. If you are past your 'teens, such a reserve of subconscious knowledge is there. Since you assigned to your inner mind a positive project, it will play back stepped-up positive influence. "What to do and when" will become energized, positive action. Through self-influence, you will have learned to use knowledge that is more powerful than the problem.

• Knowledge attracts opportunities

The "opportunity" can be treated in the same manner. First, "conscious observation" will reveal the elemental facts about the opportunity. You will define the changes that could come in your life and the personal preparation you will have to make to take advantage of the opportunity. You will define exactly what the opportunity amounts to, morally, economically, and progressively. All of this is workable knowledge. Continuing just as deliberately, you will determine what your first moves must be to capture this opportunity. This is serviceable knowledge that tells you what to do. Assign this knowledge and your intentions to your subconscious and it will add the power of stored-up knowledge and experience that will send you into action perfectly prepared. If this opportunity is right for you, then there is a reserve of subconscious knowledge that has made you ready for the opportunity. Through self-influence, you will have learned all you need to know to guide you into positive action as a claimant of this opportunity. You will claim it while it is ripe and ready!

• Knowledge and self-influence are good partners

Between these extremes of "problems" and "opportunities" are all of the other factors of everyday living, where knowing what to do and when are vital. Here, too, self-influenced concentration on knowledge of each circumstance is the basis for learning what to do. Conscious observation of facts, assignment of this knowledge to your subconscious and action based upon controlled positive influence will result in "the best" outcomes. Learning what to do, in any circumstance, through concentration on conscious and subconscious knowledge, puts you in control of your actions!

There is another facet to knowledge and learning, a technique that supports the positive pattern of the life you are building for yourself. This has to do with the kind of knowledge that comes your way, and it is aimed at putting "higher voltage" in the power of your subconscious.

• Knowledge is storing up in your subconscious

I am sure that you will agree that you learn something every day. It is always knowledge you deliberately acquired . . . or knowledge which is incidental to the day's activity. The latter is popularly called "experience." During your experience with this book, each day is providing more than your normal supply of deliberately acquired knowledge. This kind of knowledge is certainly increasing the power of your subconscious. This kind of knowledge is certainly basic to that positive pattern of life for you. More and more, you are learning what to do, and when. The significant fact is that this particular kind of knowledge is doing the trick.

Now, let's consider what is happening to all this kind of knowledge. Some of it, of course, you are putting to immediate use. Some of it is being related to goals that have to do with your future. But some of this knowledge you are acquiring purely on *speculation*. The technique of relating the knowledge to goals and to speculation is what we want to develop here.

• All positive knowledge you acquire will be used

Using the knowledge from your book is a technique parallel to that described in relation to your everyday activities. You know how vitally important goals are in your life, just now, for certain goals, you are deliberately acquiring the right kind of knowledge. You must continue to do this in support of any goal you may set, at any time. If you are to know what to do, to have controlled influence as a factor, you must learn what to do by seeking the right kind of knowledge.

There is, however, knowledge that is neither put to immediate use nor directly related to a goal. It is knowledge which you acquire speculatively, storing it away in your subconscious memory, for future use. As with your book, this speculative knowledge should be the positive kind.

Why is this speculative knowledge important? Because nothing you ever learn is ever wasted. As you have learned, it is all stored away subconsciously. Therefore any positive knowledge that you acquire, regardless of whether it is put to immediate use, will serve a good purpose some day. Inevitably, this will come at a time when you need it most. Therefore, in addition to knowledge for everyday use and for specific goals, you should be piling up knowledge speculatively, positive knowledge for that "rainy day." This technique will crowd out casual learning that tends to be negative or inconclusive. It will stimulate you and put more power in your hands. The subconscious mind loves a master who keeps pumping in positive knowledge, and the odds in favor of knowing "what to do" will get bigger and bigger!

• Go after positive knowledge consistently

Deliberately acquired positive knowledge is the key to knowing what to do, and when in any circumstance in your life. This applies to your vocational life, home life, social life, community life. Good books, objective observation of the lives of others, classes, lectures, guided home-study are all sources of the right kind of knowledge, and they are easily and constantly available to you. Knowledge acquired this way will supply more go-power no matter what your age or environment. Your willing partner, your subconscious mind, is willing to prove all of this to you. Don't pass up this opportunity, ever!

IN SUM

Your subconscious thrives on knowledge.

In dealing with a condition of life, whether it be a problem or an opportunity, consciously observe its traits.

Then decide how you must deal with the condition.

Assign your knowledge, and your intention to act, to your subconscious.

With its reserve of knowledge, your subconscious will then come to your aid.

o→ RESULT-GETTING PROJECTS ←o

1. Isolate a problem that has been buzzing around in your life like an annoying fly, and put this question alongside of it: "What should I do, and when?" Subject the problem to "conscious observation"; scrutinize it carefully until you have brushed aside all the "ifs" and found the basic truth about it. With this knowledge, define the best action you can take to solve the problem. Assign this positive knowledge to your subconscious and anticipate action within twenty-four hours. Through this self-influence. you will teach yourself to do the "right thing at the right time," and the right answer will come.

2. Put the spotlight of your interest on an opportunity that has been dangling in front of you, and label it with the question: "What should I do, and when?" Get the facts about it into that spotlight, and with practical knowledge, define the obvious best moves for you to make. Assign this positive knowledge to your subconscious; anticipate that you will know what to do. Your subconscious will provide the needed urge to act the right way at the right time.

3. Formulate a plan for deliberately acquiring positive knowledge beyond the good start you have made through this book. Include in this plan the learning of serviceable knowledge that will strongly support your goals in life. Make your plan comprehensive enough so that plenty of positive knowledge will be acquired as reserve power as it is stored in your subconscious. You can afford to "speculate" on learning *anything* that has a positive slant. Get a first draft of the learning plan down on paper right now. You'll do some polishing and perfecting of it as time goes on.

Tonight, just before you go to sleep, deliberately assign Project Number 1 to your subconscious. A written memo that you can refer to, detailing your knowledge of the problem, will be helpful. Do this tonight, and anticipate the "magic" of this knowledge prompting you to *act* tomorrow!

Tomorrow night, assign Project Number 2 to your subconscious, in the same manner, and anticipate progressive action the next day, based upon the application of the positive knowledge.

On the following night, assign Project Number 3 to your subconscious in the same way. That plan of yours for continued learning is down on paper, of course, so read and re-read it at bedtime. The desire to support that plan will be aided and abetted by the desire of your subconscious to receive and record knowledge, forever and anon!

21

You and Your Subconscious Mind as Partners in Action ... in Relation to Goals in Life

ONE OF THE MOST ABUSED AND MALIGNED WORDS IN OUR language is "budget." About money and budgets, we might say that "some people do" and "some people don't." Among those who do, there are many who budget and like it, and there are others who do it and hate it! Among those who do not, are people who say it just won't work or it isn't worth it. As with politics, people are inclined to be violently pro or con about budgets and money. Right now, I am not inviting you to make a declaration of opinion on the subject. Not as far as money is concerned, anyway. But there is another type of budget that I believe calls for positive support by you, so hold on a moment!

• The most important budget in the world

Whether we are formal budgeters with money or not we will have to agree on one fact about that cold, practical stuff. That is, we each have just so much money passing through our hands, and we have many needs and desires that require money. We are always concerned about keeping the two sides in balance. Since there is always just "so much" money, the practical angle is not how *much* we spend, but simply how we spend it and what value we get from that "so much" money. Whether the bank statement can be reconciled is not as important as what each check represents in "value received." Your "creed" and "three rules" will help materially if you are concerned about the monetary side of budgeting. But there is another slant to budgeting, a concept of it that you can't afford not to be concerned with. That is the budgeting of your life!

• Do you get value received from what you do?

Your life and the pattern of monetary income and outgo have a remarkably close parallel in the way they operate. And the *effect* of a budgeting program on both is remarkably parallel in terms of measuring value received. Look at it this way: as with money, you have just "so much" of life. The time element in your life is like income. As with money, there are many needs and desires that you want to be satisfied within that time element. The needs and desires in your life are like the outgo or the spending of money. You are concerned with keeping the two sides of life in balance. Again as with money, the important factor is not that somehow you can account for every minute of your time but rather that you get value received from what you do and how you do it. And finally, as with money, the net value depends upon your outlook on budgeting, on how

you budget your life. What you get out of life does depend
upon how you budget it.

• Budget your life

Budget your life? Yes! Budget it with goals, goals that define
and determine how you will spend that income that is the span
of your life!

Goals established in your life, goals supported with step-by-
step planning, goals worked on consistently will determine
whether you have budgeted your life so that you get the
greatest "value received" from each day, each month, each
year.

You know that influence of one kind or another is always
making demands on your time. You know that influence is
determining what you do, and what you do determines whether
each ticked-off minute is labeled worthwhile or wasted. You
know this choice of values is largely determined by the degree
of self-influence you exert over time and action. And I am
sure that you realize fully that established goals are tools of
self-influence. Therefore, I am sure that increased skill in
budgeting your life is something you want to cultivate to the
highest degree. With the help of the power of your subconscious mind, and the application of plans, you can budget your
life, and "like it!"

• This way to achievement

First, I am going to give you six "goal makers" that have
been tested and proved by thousands of graduates of the Simmons Institute. You won't need to take notes here, because I
am giving this "super six" so that you can always use these
pages as a reference. These "goal makers" are going to make
"budgeting" a pleasure!

• Major goals first

1. Establish positive, progressive goals! Relate your goals to your needs and desires to give them a positive slant. Establish goals that will take you forward from where you are, toward achievements that you can clearly define. This will label them as progressive. They become your major goals.

• Alternate goals are important

2. Establish alternate goals along with the major ones. Set up alternate objectives, similar to the major goals, which you may switch to anywhere along the line without losing ground if circumstances require a change. For example, if a major goal is a trip around the world, and your vocational status changes so that you don't have enough time to spare, go to Hawaii or Europe instead. With alternate goals established, you will go somewhere stimulating and exciting. You won't stay home, sore at the world and your job because you couldn't make it around the world! Maybe you don't want to go around the world. But whatever your major goals are, be sure that they are supported with alternates, so that progressive accomplishment is always assured.

• Timetables for progress

3. As soon as each goal is established, put a timetable alongside of it. This is where many fall by the wayside in money budgeting. This phase of budgeting is too practical for them and, while they *say* they will spend so much for this or that, they end up not doing it, because they were not definite about their goals. So, be definite about the timetable of "what, how, when." Besides, your subconscious is depending on you to be definite. It wants *specifics* to work on.

• Never turn back

4. Anticipate meeting obstacles, but also anticipate overcoming them. At any time along your way toward a goal, you may meet an obstacle that seems like "the end of the road" or that appears to say: "You're all wrong! Forget the whole idea!" Don't let either throw you. Get a good strong grip on the progress you have made, and hold that position! Hold it until you can thoroughly evaluate the circumstance and determine how to overcome the obstacle. You can overcome it. Remember the chapter on knowledge and learning? That told you how to meet such a situation. The important thing is to keep the goal strongly in focus and don't turn back.

• Variety is necessary

5. Budget your life with a variety of goals. Remember that your subconscious is your partner here, and this partner thrives on variety. The "more the merrier" is the way your subconscious looks at goals. One goal at a time won't amount to an adequate "budget" anyway. The important factor is have several different kinds of goals on the list at the same time.

• Sell your goals to others

6. Let everyone who should know be aware that you have established your goals and that "this is your life" as far as action is concerned. Much of your action in relation to goals is dependent upon your relationship with others. People like to be associated with stimulating, progressive action. They will help you along the way, if you ask them to. Try it!

Use the six "goal makers" and your skill in budgeting your life will increase day-by-day. Now I am going to add just one more "slant" to this plan. It is most closely related to your "timetable," but it also transcends all of the other five steps. This will become quite obvious to you once you are in action on your goals. It is that your goals are dynamic things. There must be, as in your life, an element of flexibility in their use. This will be taken care of if you have goals for today, goals for the coming week, month, year, as well as goals for your total life. Obviously some of the goals for today are really progress steps in the goals for the coming month or year. The important factor in budgeting, here, is that action toward your goals is progressive only when you relate them to the progress of time. This concept can make every day a "red letter day" for you, because you are always doing something new in relation to your goals. This will make a mighty interesting life, if you budget this way!

• Goals must be hand-made

There is something stimulating and compelling about these "goal makers," isn't there? That's because they were custom made to fit the "creed" and the "three rules," which are becoming such major factors in your life. But even beyond that, they typify the kind of action that best uses the power of your subconscious. Goals are really "targets" in your life, and the only way to consistently score a bull's-eye on those targets is to keep your "sights" on them and keep firing! Goals consciously established according to this plan will become bull's-eyes that your subconscious will influence you to keep in sight, always. Budgeting your life, with your subconscious as your stimulating partner, will become a matter of standard procedure with you.

Specifically what should your goals be? If this is not clear to you at this point, you know where to find the answers. They are in Chapters 5, 6 and 7, and Chapters 14, 15 and 16. The answers are in the analysis you have made of your life, and in the practice steps you have taken.

You need now to boldly establish those positive, progressive goals, and assign them to your subconscious as the way you want your life to be budgeted!

IN SUM

Budget your life.
This is to say that you must establish goals that will give you the greatest value every day of your life.

---

o→ RESULT-GETTING PROJECT ←o

This project, recommended to be of several days duration, will induce the skill of "budgeting through goals."

Step 1. Set aside a time of the day or night when you can establish the atmosphere of a "retreat" for yourself, where your body is relaxed and you are at ease and where your conscious mind can concentrate on your "budget." A retreat, as you know, invites your subconscious to be an alert observer of your conscious thoughts and actions. Since this is going to be a positive action on your part, it will establish an ideal relationship with your subconscious. While you are thus "in retreat," make a list of your goals, as you are able to identify them at this time. Write them down just as you think of them. Take your time, ponder over each item until you can make a clear statement about it. Little goals, big goals, get them on the first draft of this budget. That's all this is at the moment, a first draft. But do make it complete, covering all of your needs, desires, aspirations. It should be quite a *long* list! The very act of making this list is giving a command to your subconscious to do something about the goals. On the first night after this retreat, make the command even stronger, by reading and reviewing the list just before you go to sleep. Let the contents be the important thoughts. The next day their importance will be increased. Now you are ready for Step 2!

Step 2. Established another time of retreat for yourself. Take your list with you, plus paper for your timetable. With the preparatory work you have consciously and subconsciously done to set the stage, you will find that putting a date of achievement on each goal seems to happen "just naturally." Being intelligently practical about it, having not the slightest doubt as to the validity of your action, say about each goal: "This is when I plan to achieve it!" And put down a date. Obviously, this is going to put some time priorities on your new list, and you will end up with goals for the week, the month, the year, and even beyond. Stay with it, because now is when the list becomes a "budget of life." Put an alternate goal alongside of each major goal. List at least the first two or three action steps you will take in relation to each goal. Put a tentative date on each step. Now you really have a "budget of life," don't you? Just one more thing and you will be finished with this session. Make a list of each action step in a one-week period, beginning, say the day after tomorrow. Tonight, at bedtime, assign this one-week budget to your subconscious.

Step 3. The following day, spend another few minutes polishing up the one-week budget. Get the coming week's progressive plan all ready to go! Visualize it, this way: you are getting ready to go to a big party. It's going to be a wonderful affair, exciting, with lots doing! You are all primed for it, and you can hardly wait for tomorrow! With this attitude, take the polished one-week budget to bed with you. Your subconscious will then be as well prepared for the big day, just as your conscious being is. The next morning, nothing will stop you from putting this first-class budget into action!

22

You and Your Subconscious Mind as Partners in Action ... in Relation to Success

ALMOST EVERYBODY LIKES TO READ "SUCCESS STORIES." I suggest that you read the stories of people who have lived eminently successful lives. I have always recommended the reading of biographies to my students. The reason I encourage such reading and the reason the majority of people read "success stories," I have found from experience, are often at considerable variance. I do not condemn those who do not read them objectively, which is my reason, but I do feel that they are passing up an opportunity to get several times the value than comes from simply reading them romantically.

• Success is true romance

Do I sound as though I am being a profound moralist and
saying that you shouldn't read just for the sheer pleasure of it?
I assure you that that is not my viewpoint. There is romance in
success and in stories about success. Success in anyone's life
is romance of the highest order, and it should be this way in
your life.

Let me amplify my viewpoint because it can change your
interpretation of "success stories" to your advantage. I want
to encourage you to find the "behind-the-scenes" facts about
success stories that will be far more stimulating than any
melodramatic or extravagant "happy ending." If you could read
a success story about a person, without knowing in advance
who the person was, or what the "happy ending" was, you
would read much differently and have a more objective viewpoint. If the hero was anonymous until the end, you would see
him as a person not unlike yourself, with similar needs and
desires and with a similar pattern of problems and opportunities in his life. But more than that, I am sure you would see
that success came to him not because he was specially blessed
and set apart by Providence, but because of what he did, based
upon a self-influenced life.

• Before success

Unfortunately we don't find biographies written that way; as
a consequence, the private thought of most people reading a
biography are: "Well, of course things happened like this to
that person! Just look at who he, or she was!" Nonsense! Of
course, "look at who he or she was" *after* success put them in
the spotlight. But more important, look at who they were
before they became "hero" or "heroine"; look at them when

they were at the bottom of the ladder and while they were working their way up! Look at the lives of successful people during those periods and you will find the real story of success, the story that is important to you.

• Success can be made to happen to you

Remember the list of successful people we met in Chapter 3? Things didn't "happen" to those people just because they had those names. You wouldn't know they even existed if it wasn't for what they did to make things happen. Making things happen, with self-influenced control, was what made them successful. This is so of every successful person, and it will be so for you! Therefore your success story is to be based upon making things happen that will result in achievements. You and I can visualize the "happy ending" that will characterize your biography. But most important is what happens between now and then. If your success story is to be written, it must tell of a lot of achievements, many things carried through to a good conclusion and much recognition along the way.

So, what is the definition of a successful person? It is one who takes his or her goals through to a successful conclusion, by making things happen.

• Don't compromise with failure

At this point, let's consider a compromise viewpoint of success that is so common among "average" people. What do you think would happen if you were to say to a friend: "Since you are not a success, you must be a failure!" With an insult like that, you wouldn't expect to have him or her for a friend any longer. But suppose you and the other person could stay on an even keel, what do you think his follow-up would be? Perhaps, if you were your friend, you would say: "I know what I would say!" (If your reply is anything like what follows, I want you to figure on a quick change!)

Most would reply: "Oh, I'll admit I haven't made a big success of things, but I certainly don't think I'm a failure! I could do better, but I get along!" With this attitude, people assign *themselves* to a never-never land between success and failure. They seem to be able to do enough to keep their heads above water. They "get along" by letting things happen to them. They wouldn't mind holding a winning ticket in what they call the "lottery of life." They seem unwilling to make an investment in success by making things happen. They don't reach the point of wanting to "end it all," but for them too much of the time, life isn't "worth living."

• Not who you are, but what you do

Are these people successful in life? Obviously not! But are they failures? No, not in the sense that they were predestined to live compromised lives. No one is a failure until he says he is. But by *not* saying he is or will be a success, he is assigning himself to that purgatory where success is always for somebody else. All of this points up one dramatically significant fact—you can't say about those people: "*Of course* things happen as they do to them. Just look at who they are!" You can't say that it is true of them any more than it is true of successful people.

You can say that successful people make things happen in relation to their goals, while those who compromise with life just let things happen and their goals remain daydreams. At any time, any person can start writing his own success story, no matter what his past record had been. As for yourself, you are already writing the first chapter in your success story through your experiences with this book of *yours*. Consider how true this is.

You have taken many practice steps in the use of subconscious self-influence. You have been involved in action that has resulted in desirable outcomes in your life. The self-influenced planning and the self-influenced action in each step resulted in an experience with achievement. In these experiences you have been a success, and my hat is off to you! You have proved this yourself: Established goals, plus "making things happen," equals success!

• Success is for today

Success is a lot of achievements, everyday achievements, achievements gained by deliberately making things happen. Success means following through to a good conclusion on every goal you set up. There is no other way to be successful! Success comes from putting your goals into action, step by step. Each time you take a first step toward a goal, it is an achievement! It is an achievement when you take the second step, and the third and every step, until you have reached a goal.

Since you have made this good start, continue with your success story by making things happen in acordance with the way you have budgeted your life. If you need to strengthen your attitude toward this positive action, go back and review Chapters 11 and 13. And always remember this: your subconscious mind is the co-author of your success story. It will make your success story colorful and exciting, if you will condition it to influence you to act so that many achievements —every day achievements that come from self-influenced action—come your way.

Success? Of course! In the proper abundance that befits a person who has established his or her importance in the scheme of things. That is you, isn't it?

IN SUM

A successful person is one who deliberately makes things happen.
He is one who takes action to achieve his goals.

---

o→   RESULT-GETTING PROJECT   ←o

Confirm your status in the ranks of those who are successful by giving recognition to your achievements. *Recognition*, as you know, is a powerful factor in life. This project will give you that conscious recognition that you deserve for your success achievements. But it will do much more. It is intended to impress upon your subconscious the fact that "making things happen" to bring achievement is the way you want things to continue to happen. So, set up a scoreboard of achievements that have been yours, and keep adding to the scoreboard, day by day.

You can make a good start by considering what you have done with your practice projects in this book. And don't think this idea of an accomplishment chart is "kid stuff." It's "adult stuff" and it really works. Take a look at success in your life and know that you are on the right road!

This scoreboard should be a piece of paper with three columns on it. The first column lists the actions involved in your practice steps (or in any other action where *you* planned the steps). The second column is headed "Planned" and the third column "Achieved." List everything you can think of that you "planned" and "achieved" and put a check mark after each item in both columns. Now list the goals that you have set before you. Check them off in the "planned" column. As fast as you make an achievement in relation to any goal, or any step toward that goal, mark it in the "achieved" column.

What are you accomplishing by checking off items in the third column? First of all, you are proving that you have been successful in the many instances where you made things happen. Second, you are proving that each time you make something happen that you planned, you are successful. And third, you see that ahead of you are more achievements and more success as you continue to make things happen. This is the pattern of life for a successful person, you!

23

You and Your Subconscious Mind as Partners in Action ... in Relation to Happiness

BRIDES ARE REPUTED TO SAY, AFTER THE NUPTIAL CEREmony: "This is the happiest moment of my life!" Parents are credited with saying, upon their child's graduation: "This is our happiest moment!" So-called "strong" men are inclined to say upon receipt of some signal honor: "I am grateful for this honor. This is the happiest moment of my life." In one form or another, I am sure you often hear people say rather impetuously: "This is the happiest moment of my life!" Usually, the statement is emotionally impelled by reason of some dramatic circumstance. I am one hundred per cent for spontaneous reaction to joyful moments. There can't be too many of them as far as I am concerned, but I do take exception to labeling any one moment in life as the happiest moment, because life would be a pretty sad affair for anyone who had already had his or her "happiest moment" and had none as good to look forward to!

• Happiness should not be exceptional

I am pretty sure that you are inclined to remind me that people don't mean it literally when they say, "This is my happiest moment." Yes, I know. They mean to say that a certain event is one of their happiest moments. But there is something else that most of these people mean. They are implying that such events of great happiness are exceptional in their lives. *That* should not be so, for them, for you or for anyone.

Because of all of the opportunities there are for being happy, and because you can consistently make choices of activities that induce happiness, there is no reason for this desirable circumstance to be exceptional for you. Such opportunities are abundant in your daily life, and such choices are yours to make. You only have to set the stage for such influences to be effective, which simply means self-influenced action that is branded with "happiness."

• What is happiness?

Let's see if we can define happiness in a down-to-earth, practical manner. Once it is thus defined, it will be easier to establish it as a usual, everyday condition rather than as an exceptional circumstance. I feel sure that these definitions will fit your feeling of what happiness really is.

You are happy when you feel right about yourself, about others, about your environment, about your lot in life. Let's broaden that idea a bit and see how close it comes to the time when you are happy. First, let me say that I agree with you in your observation that happiness has many outward manifestations. When you are happy, you are cheerful, or joyful, or genial, or optimistic, or contented, or just in good humor. But actually these are the results of being happy, are they not?

• Actions bring happiness

If you do something that is creative, and as a result you produce something distinctive, you feel right about yourself. This puts you in good humor, and you are optimistic about success, so you are happy, about yourself. If you work with someone on a project that brings enjoyment to both of you, you feel right about this other person. Because you are genial, and share this good experience with another person, you feel right about the whole idea, and you are happy! If, in relation to your family, your associates at work, a social group, you do something to better their lot, you feel right about your environment, and you are happy to be a part of it.

Pause a moment, and consider the times when you have felt right about yourself, or about the people and things around you. Those were times that you were really happy, weren't they? And if you analyze those times further, you find that they happened when you did something that brought them about. YOU, *personally*, did something! So, one practical definition of happiness is: feeling right as the result of doing something genial, or cheerful, or optimistic. There are unlimited opportunities in your daily life for doing such things, provided you choose to do them!

Happiness is like a warm fire, a warming influence that you need in your life, but like a fire, happiness needs fuel. There is fuel in abundance all around you. Gather it in and use it, and you don't have to let that warming fire ever go out of your life. In a moment, I'll show you how to be an expert "fire tender" without having to do anything that you wouldn't want to do.

• Happiness pays life-long dividends

Consider one other factor about happiness. This, too, is in relation to your own life. Happiness is made up partly of current experiences and partly of memories. As a result, anything that you do today that makes you feel right, and brings happiness, will have a lasting effect in the form of a happy memory. A store of happy memories is like a treasure. You can keep them forever and they will always have value. In fact, they will increase in value, as attested by those who have but a few memories of those "happiest moments."

• Make happiness a habit

All of this is most significant to you, because your subconscious is the storehouse for these memories; if you have an abundant supply of them stored away there, you are going to be more and more influenced by them. It is apparent, therefore, that everything you do today and in the future that makes you feel right and happy will increase the influence for happiness that comes from the power of your subconscious. Does this imply that happiness can become a habit? It does, and the time to start cultivating that habit through self-influence is now. How? This way:

• Happiness is giving

1. Give of yourself. Give of your talents, your abilities, your time, in a service relationship to others. Start with those closest to you, your family, your friends. Expand your "giving" to your working associates, to community groups. Support others through your physical, moral and spiritual efforts. Be service-

minded service-motivated, and you will feel right and be happy!

• Happiness is seeing right

2. Look for the bright side. Every circumstance and every relationship does have two sides to it, and one side is a bright side! Look for it! Impractical? A Pollyanna? Not at all! "The creed" and "three rules" that are the basis of controlled self-influence tell you that the only answers for you are on the bright side! The bright side of things and of people is the optimistic, cheerful side, and if, at first, this side is not apparent, search for it. You don't want to see the dark side of things, do you? Of course not! To feel right, see right, be right and be happy, do what you want to do, look for the bright side until you find it.

• Happiness is acting positively

3. Act purposefully. This is one of the major themes of your book. All we are doing here is re-emphasizing that if you want to feel right, and be happy, you can't be passive. You will attract happiness to yourself as though you are a magnet only through purposeful action. Every time you act purposefully, you are knocking out fear, doubt and uncertainty. Your practice projects with self-influence have proven that, because you felt right about every one of them. Purposeful action brings about optimism and contentment. As a result, you can't feel "righter" or happier!

• Happiness is living your faith

4. Establish and maintain a working relationship with your God. It is not within my province to prescribe the ways and

means of your relationship with your God, or to recommend a specific doctrine or church or religious union. Whatever your choice is in this matter, I know that it is the right one for you. What I do recommend is a working relationship. Be an active participant in whatever action will support your religious faith, and live your faith as though it were as much a part of your every day life as eating, working, sleeping. "Feeling right" once a week through attendance at a worship service is good, but it's like a starvation diet! Seven days a week should be standard for feeling right about your relationship to your God. The answer is a working relationship, and happiness.

• Happiness is harmonious action

5. Seek peace of mind. Peace of mind is not an elusive thing. It is maintained by keeping your emotional reactions and your physical reactions on an even keel, together. This is done by cultivating an attitude of personal inner harmony that says in the face of disturbing environmental conditions, "This negative condition is not good, I see that clearly. I can do something positive to offset it. That too, I see clearly, and I will do it at once!" This implies that harmony is a dynamic force, doesn't it? That it is! It is the substitution of a positive reaction for a negative one, a power you possess with the help of your subconscious. The kind of dynamic harmony that is the key to peace of mind, to feeling right and to happiness.

All of these add up to a grass-roots interpretation of happiness. There is nothing superficial or artificial about them. The important point is that all of them are actions based upon self-influence . . . and upon things that you really want to do. None of them has anything to do with any "special occasion" or "exceptional moment." You can do every one of them every day! You know that the opportunities are in plentiful supply and, above all, you know that the choice is up to you. So, as you are now skilled in self-influenced action, the answer is quite obvious. These are the things you will do to feel right, and be happy!

IN SUM

A happy person is one who deliberately makes things happen.

He takes advantage of the unlimited daily opportunities for giving of himself.

He looks for the bright side.

He acts purposefully, living his faith and seeking peace of mind.

---

o➤ RESULT-GETTING PROJECTS ◄o

The "habit of happiness" starts with the self-influenced attitude of "What I do will bring me happiness, what I can do will bring me happiness, what I will do will bring me happiness." Assign this declaration to your subconscious along with any other projects you are working on. For example, if you are working on projects in relation to faith or goals, *add* this declaration of intention to the other work you are doing for yourself, consciously and subconsciously. Don't isolate this assignment as something too "special." It is important. But remember, we don't want happiness to be an exceptional condition. We want to get it established as a usual condition. So get this step into your program as though it belonged there no matter what else is going on.

So, first establish the attitude of "I do, I can, I will." Then, choose a day, a full day, when you will deliberately do at least one thing in line with each of the actions that make you feel right and happy.

Use the "timetable" based upon your goals and, within the coming week, get this day established on the "timetable." Here is something that is most important, and with a slightly different angle to it. *Don't* try to establish the specific things you will do, but set up as goals, the kinds of things you will do, give of yourself, look on the bright side, act purposefully, demonstrate a working relationship with your God, and seek peace of mind through harmonious actions. Having determined to do these kinds of things, *look for opportunities* to do them on the chosen day. For example, you won't know in advance "where and what" you are going to look for to find the bright side. All you know in advance is that you are going to look for the opportunity to do it, and then act accordingly. The opportunity will present itself!

This is the second step in establishing the "habit of happiness." Having done them on a chosen day—which is to be one of your regular, active days—you will prove that there is nothing "exceptional" about happy experiences, since the same thing can happen every day! Be sure of this: identify these kinds of actions to your subconscious, as a preliminary to each day, until the "habit of happiness" is established!

24

You and Your Subconscious Mind as Partners in Action . . . in Relation to Heredity and Environment

"HE WAS BORN THAT WAY. HE COULDN'T BE ANY DIFFERENT if he tried!" You have heard descriptions like that defining some outstanding trait in a person.

"What else could you expect? Look at the conditions in her home. You would be the same way, if you were in her shoes." You have also heard comments like these when some person's life is being described.

These remarks represent generalizations about the influence of heredity and environment that have been too commonly accepted. The first would indicate that a person was born with his life inevitably mapped out, with no chance for deviation. The others would indicate that a person's environment is the major influence in his life, regardless of other factors. There is an apparent conflict in this philosophy of life or, at the least, there could be for those who apparently believe those generalized statements. If either has been your belief in the past, I am sure that you now know that neither statement should be taken as the basic truth.

• Twin influences in your life

In fact, I believe that you could write this chapter yourself, insofar as the application of the title is concerned with the contents of this book about you. You are now well aware of most of the basic inheritances that are yours. You know what to look for in the power of influence from these inheritances. You are aware of the power of influence from your environment. You are coming closer and closer to the ability to control the power of both of these influences. You have been plotting this control and practicing it, and all of it adds up to action in relation to your heredity and environment. That story about you certainly would fit this chapter heading, wouldn't it?

I want to add a bit to your contribution to this chapter and I am only able to do it in the way I am taking, because of the knowledge and experience you have had with influence control up to the present. I want to be sure that heredity and environment are always *positive* factors in your life, particularly if there has been any tendency toward either of them having been a negative factor in the past.

Books by the thousands have been written about heredity and environment. Educational institutions, teachers, researchers and scholars have devoted years to the study and interpretation of the subjects. Professionals in the fields of medicine, psychology, psychiatry, religion, health and social welfare are concerned with these subjects. All this attests to the importance of the "cause and effect" of heredity and environment.

In a very realistic way, this book is a summation of certain accumulated knowledge of the subject, knowledge based upon these "cause and effect" studies. I want to pin-point certain factors of heredity and environment as they relate to your life and to subconscious self-influence.

• Which one governs your life?

Many people, including scholars, line themselves up rather vehemently on either side of this matter. Some claim that heredity is the strongest factor, while others claim that environment is the predominant one. I must respectfully disagree with those who say that either one is more potent and say that I believe neither is more important, that both are powerful factors. Yes, both are powerful influences and both materially affect the life of a person. But both are subject to control by the person who practices self-influence. Our objective here is to prove that neither needs to be an inevitable, uncontrolled force in your life, particularly if a negative influence has been exerted.

• The influence of heredity

Let's examine some of the facts of heredity as they might affect you and your use of self-influence. Certainly we understand the effect of the biological inheritance of genes that is part of the parent-offspring relationship. Physical and personality traits often appear to be passed along from generation to generation, through the persistence of certain genes in a family line. Sometimes these are so pronounced among members of a family, that people will say of a particular person: "You can certainly tell that he is a "Smith," or, "She is just like her mother." Many families take pride in this transfer of traits and consider them marks of distinction. On the other hand, some families consider their inheritance of certain traits as a curse. Still further, an anomaly will occasionally appear in a family line, a non-conformist who doesn't follow the hereditary pattern. Among families who take pride in heredity, such a person is often called a "black sheep." An anomaly in another family is credited with "rising above" his heredity. It would appear, in the face of all this, that either you "do or you don't," either you "have or have not," in the matter of inherited traits, and that whatever you have been given is setting an inevitable pattern. If you accept this as gospel, you are accepting only half of the facts.

• Many positive inheritances

Certainly, the transfer of genes and personality traits is something you can't control, but to a great degree you can control or amend the *effects* of them. You can capitalize on the positive traits, and you can minimize the negative ones. This is possible because of some of the facts about yourself, concerning some other inheritances that you arealready aware of. First, you were born with the fundamental urges, about which we have been concerned all the way along in your book. Among these are the urge for self-expression, progressiveness, recognition, adventure. Second, you were also born with certain marks of distinctiveness that make you a unique individual. These inheritances are from your creator, and you know that you can and will use them to the best advantage through your program of self-influence.

Now, let's juxtapose these two phases of hereditary action and compare them with the theory of self-control of your life. Let's do it, for example, by considering two common hereditary traits: the trait that makes one person an introvert and the

trait that makes another an extrovert. Actually neither is undesirable except when allowed to become *extreme* influences. A
combination of both, in the right proportions, is ideal.

• Heredity factors under control

A person who has inherited the trait of extreme introversion
could be considered to be "cursed" if he lets it make a captive
of him. Uncontrolled, this tendency causes him to hold back, to
withdraw within himself, to live passively instead of dynamically. But if the same person, through self-influence, unleashes
the fundamental urges he has and capitalizes on his distinctiveness, he can make an asset out of his Introversion. It becomes
an asset when he looks at himself and his life objectively, which
is "a natural" for him, since he has the inherited capacity to
think things through. It becomes an asset when he plans his
life carefully, which is also an inherited ability he possesses.
With the ability to do these vital things so superbly, the introvert can put himself in an ideal circumstance to use subconscious self-influence for action based upon the best that is
in him. He thus converts a potentially negative hereditary
factor into a positive one. Thus, through the use of the "creed"
and the "three rules" of self-control, he creates the proper
proportion of extroversion in his life.

The person who apparently has inherited the trait of extreme extraversion can be considered equally "cursed" if the
trait tends to take him through life like a runaway horse. The
person who tends to "act before he thinks" too often makes
himself and others unhappy. Often such a person tends to
rationalize his unbridled actions as "something he can't help."
He becomes an expert at recovering from self-made, undesirable situations. All of this is wasted time and energy, because
of the lack of purposefulness and control.

However, this kind of a person has the potential for a fine life because dynamic action comes naturally to him. His need is to consider those fundamental urges of his, and his distinctiveness, as the objects of his dynamic energy. This he can do through the use of the same "creed," and the same "three rules," plus self-influenced planning. In fact, such a person finds great stimulation in the self-influenced planning of his life, because he can clearly picture himself in action. He is used to action! Every time this person plans something, the plans have a "lighted fuse" attached to them, because action is what he wants out of life. By first directing his action to objective planning, this person puts himself in the right position to use subconscious self-influence to cause the best action. Thus he creates the proper proportion of introversion in his life, and he converts his inherited extroversion into a fine asset.

• Self-control is stronger influence

The same pattern of control is applicable to any hereditary personality trait. Those which are positively slanted can be used to greatest advantage through self-controlled action. Those which tend to be negative can be minimized or converted to positive helps, through the increase of the power of the fundamental urges and personal distinctiveness, and through self-controlled action. Thus there is no pattern of the inevitable in hereditary factors in your life, since their influence is subject to subconscious self-control.

• Environmental factors under control

We do not need to dwell on the facts of environmental influence. Through your experiences with your book, you know that such outside influences can be put into a controlled relationship with your life. You know that there is no inevitable pattern in environmental influences, for you. In view of *this* knowledge, plus some of the facts about heredity we have just discussed, is one, or any of the other, of these factors most important in your life? All are important, and all can and need to be subject to self-influenced control on your part.

• Choose the best of each

There is no "curse" in hereditary factors unless you let them become uncontrolled. You are not a "black sheep" if you go contrary to a hereditary pattern, if that pattern by itself does not provide a positive life for you. There need not be a predestined life because of undesirable environmental factors. The obligation you have to yourself is that you frankly recognize all of the hereditary traits you possess and "play up" the best ones and "play down" the questionable ones, through self-controlled action. Your obligation also is to frankly identify all of the environmental factors that surround you, to use the best of them and to substitute positive factors for any negative ones that exist. And this, too, you can do through self-influenced action.

Through subconscious self-influence, as applied to your life through the principles of our "creed" and the "three rules," you will recognize the importance of heredity and environment as major influences, but you will give them their proper importance in relation to your planned life.

Perhaps this is an appropriate moment to go back and re-read Chapter 1, "What Is Life?" I believe that the re-reading of the section now, will strengthen your understanding of the true values of heredity and environment in your life.

IN SUM

Inherited and environmental factors do not have an absolute control over your life.

Recognize those factors.

Through self-influence, use the positive factors and substitute for the negative ones.

o→   RESULT-GETTING PROJECT   ←o

This project is a self-inventory which will paint a picture of the cross-fire effect of heredity and environment in your life. Here is a list of ten personality elements. Copy them onto a piece of paper so that you may score each item, under a choice of four column headings. Head the columns: 1. "Good"; 2. "Need Improvement"; 3. "Heredity"; 4. "Environment."

COPY THIS LIST: 1. Personal appearance
    2. Use of good judgment
    3. Decision making
    4. Getting along with others
    5. Optimistic viewpoint
    6. Follow-through on plans
    7. Cheerfulness
    8. Influence over others
    9. Influence over self
    10. Self-expression

Now, go down the list and place each item under (1) Good or (2) Need improvement. Your experience so far with your book has proved that "honesty is the best policy," so I know that you will do this scoring on a truthful basis. Now, go back to item No. 1, Personal appearance, again, and make another decision about the item, in either column 3 or 4. Decide whether your score is "Good" or you "Need Improvement" in each item because of hereditary or environmental influences. In other words, is your score the result of a tendency you have inherited or the result of the circumstances surrounding your life?

You are not going to be able to check off the answers as though this were an ordinary questionnaire. You will find yourself carefully considering each item as you ask, "Why am I this way? Was I born this way, or did I become this way as the result of how I have lived?" When you have scored all the items in either Column 1 or 2, and in either column 3 or 4, go back to item 1 again. Put a big check mark in front of each item where you consider that your own influence over yourself has brought a score of "good." Put a big zero in front of each item where lack of self-influence has caused you to score "Need improvement." My prediction is that every item will have either a check mark or a zero in front of it. This will prove to you that if any personality factor is "Good" or "Needs improvement," it is that way because of what you do or do not do about it, regardless of whether heredity or environment is the major factor in its existence in your life.

I strongly urge you to make this self-inventory. The result will represent a concept of life that few people accept, primarily because they believe that hereditary or environmental influences have inevitable effects. They would have to be shown that this is not so. This project is aimed at showing you, because of its vital importance to you.

You and Your Subconscious Mind
as Partners in Action
. . . in Relation to Health

I AM STARTING THIS CHAPTER ON HEALTH WITH A STORY that is intended to be propaganda to influence your subconscious mind. I have a good reason for this approach, which I will tell you about later. Just now, I assure you that this will be positive propaganda, so it will make a good impression on your subconscious.

• Just a shiny penny, not a gold piece

This is the story of one single penny. Once upon a time, a storekeeper was counting his receipts at the end of the day. With a hundred or more coins spread out on the counter, he was counting and stacking halves, quarters, dimes, nickels, and finally a number of pennies. He spread them out so that he

could count them, two-by-two. Suddenly, his eye was attracted
to one shiny penny that lay like a little gold piece among all
the rest.

- **"Even as you and I . . ."**

The storekeeper paused, smiled and picked up the penny,
and he slipped it into his pocket, even as you or I might have
done. We can understand that somehow it seemed like a good
idea to hang on to that bright little coin . . . as though it
might be a symbol of good fortune. In the days after that, the
storekeeper, as you and I might do, would dig into his pocket
every so often for change and come across the penny. He would
smile and make sure he didn't spend it. It might even be said
that he became affectionate toward the little penny.

But, alas, one day it accidentally dropped from his hand
when he was putting coins into a parking meter. Unaware that
he had dropped it, he walked away, leaving the shiny penny
lying on the sidewalk. It didn't lie there for long, because a
passerby spotted it and retrieved it. It seemed like more than a
simple coin to this man, too, because of the shininess, and he
thought, "I think I'll keep it, just because it looks more valuable
than other pennies." And he did keep it, for quite some time,
until he accidentally spent it. He hoped some one else would
see its value and give it a good home. That is just what happened when a certain other man received it in change at the
store. He spotted its golden shine and had an inspiration for
using it.

- **. . . But it wasn't a new penny**

That evening, when he gave his young daughter her weekly
allowance he told her she was getting a "raise" and included
the little penny with the usual large silver coin. The little girl

saw it as something like a magic coin and said she would never spend it! She showed her treasure to her mother, who immediately had to satisify the same curiosity that you and I might have by looking at the mint date. Surprised at what she read, she exclaimed, "Why; this isn't a new penny! I wonder why it's so shiny?"

Well, her husband couldn't answer that, and neither can I, except to say that the penny had some special quality about it, something that made it look new, even though it was as old as the other pennies with the same mint date.

• Take a lesson from the penny

The point to this fable could be that no matter how old you are, it's how old others think you are that counts! But I think that a more subtle and even more important point that is displayed here is that if you want to be something special, you must look special. With the assumed license of a "modern" fable teller, I say that the second point applies to health, and that the whole fable emphasizes a significant concept of health, this concept is one that your subconscious has a great deal to do with!

Recalling the storekeeper in the story, I am sure that you can imagine the assortment of pennies he had spread out to count. This assortment could be likened to a group of people picked at random. Among the pennies you would see coins with many different appearances, just like the people in the representative group. You would see some pennies that were worn around the edges, while others would be shabby in appearance, as though they were "tired of it all." Still others would look just past the "new" stage . . . and while they wouldn't look too bad, they would be lusterless in comparison with that one shiny penny.

You know, of course, that every one of the coins is worth exactly one cent in spending value, yet the shiny one looks as if it were worth a *lot* more. You know, too, that it is still just a penny, made of the same metal as all the rest. Yet, strictly from an appearance standpoint, I am sure that your reaction to it would be the same as the people in the fable. You would see something "special" in it, and you would be attracted to it.

• Some people look bright and shiny

Now to relate all of this to health. I am sure that you can recall mental pictures of people you know who fit the descriptions of the pennies. I am equally sure that if you could get them to confess, they would tell you that they feel just as they look. If we asked the person who looks like the bright shiny penny how he or she felt, the prompt answer would be, "I feel wonderful!" From my own experience in analyzing the "inner man," I know there *is* something *special* about this person, just as with the shiny penny. But, this is where the fable and the person differ. While we said we didn't know why the not-so-new penny was special, we do know why the person is.

• Look right and you must be right

There is something "special" in a person who looks like a bright shiny penny. This is the desire to look that way, the self-influenced desire to feel right, look right, and therefore be right! This is the key to the wholesome influence of Health in your life!

• First, take care of your body

Of course, health has many facets in your life, and I urge you to be realistic about all of them. I am confident that you follow the rules of good physical health, and that you provide good care and maintenance for your body. I know that you will always do the intelligent things that will keep your body functioning as near normally as possible. And certainly, if there are times when you need professional help to correct some physical condition, you will seek that help and have faith in it.

• Adopt good mental health habits

I know that you have proper concern for your mental health. You have demonstrated that through your interest in this book of yours. Your mind is a functional element of your being which can be abused or misused, just as your muscles or your heart. Concentration on positive influences, such as you are doing now, is an important mental health factor, and I know that you will continue to follow this pattern, which is a program of good mental health.

• Provide for spiritual good health

And, of course, there is the matter of spiritual health. Spiritual health is a transitory, almost fragile condition. It requires constant "feeding" of a diet based upon faith, understanding, good will, belief in the Supreme Spirit and belief in relationships and conditions that are right for you. We have already covered all of this, so I know that spiritual good health is a positive factor in your life.

Yes, physical, mental and spiritual health are three of the major facets of health in your life. In each case I am sure that you realize the importance of maintaining the adjective "good" in relation with each of them. If this is not among the goals you have set up for yourself, then now is the time to add it to your list. But there is another fact to health, one you cannot afford to overlook. It is subconscious good health! Never heard of it? I think you have, but perhaps under a different label. In fact, I am certain that you have had casual experiences with it, at sometime in your life. Of course, you *now* know that you should never be casual about anything that has to do with your subconscious; our objective is to make subconscious good health a dynamic health factor in your life. This is the ingredient that will make you look like the shiny penny, with something "special" in its makeup.

• Subconscious support of good health

Subconscious good health is really a simple thing to develop, to have, and to hold. It is the key to having the right attitude, the positive attitude, toward physical, mental and spiritual health. It helps put the right values on these factors. It helps add the adjective "good," because it is based on a belief in good health, for yourself.

I have worked with people who have had no negative physical condition yet felt "bad." Actually, they looked as if they lacked good health. On the other hand, I have been associated with people who had serious bodily handicaps, yet they declared they "felt fine" . . . and they looked to be in perfect health. Some people apparently have the desire to "feel bad." They seem to enjoy it! All I can say is "What a life that must not be." On the other hand, some have the desire to feel good and, as a consequence, they look as though they were sitting on top of the world! That is the way for you to enjoy life!

• Look shiny, and mean it!

The way to enjoy life is to look like the bright, shiny penny. Perhaps you've heard that "folksy" description of "shiny" people. It goes like this: "You look bright-eyed and bushy-tailed." I picture a lively little squirrel when I hear that phrase, one of those little fellows who always seems to be alert and happy. At least, he looks that way. That's the key to sub-conscious good health.

You can't look "bright-eyed and bushy-tailed" unless you feel that way. It's pretty hard to maintain a false front for your feelings consistently. Therefore, if you want to look bright and healthy, and if you mean that you want to look that way, you are going to have to back up that appearance with your true feelings!

Obviously, this means simply creating the subconscious desire to look bright and shiny, to look the picture of good health. Here is a case where the proverb about a "picture being more effective than a thousand words" applies. You don't have to be concerned with formulae and rules for good health to create this powerful subconscious influence. All you have to do is create a mental picture of yourself as one who looks bright, shiny and healthy. This is a positive picture that your subconscious will support. Subconscious support of such a picture of you will induce you to act so that it becomes a real life picture.

• You look just fine!

Subconscious good health means that you see yourself as shiny and attractive as the penny in the fable. It means that you are letting the power of your subconscious influence you to actually look that way to others. This influence will cause that effect, because it will induce you to act according to concepts of good physical, mental and spiritual health. It is the ideal way for you to subconsciously picture yourself, so that is the way you will be. That's for you, isn't it?

```
┌─────────────────────────────────────────────┐
│                                               │
│                   IN SUM                       │
│                                               │
│     Subconscious good health is dependent on a positive │
│     desire for good physical, mental and spiritual health. │
│     Create the subconscious desire to look the picture │
│     of good health.                            │
│                                               │
└─────────────────────────────────────────────┘
```

o→ RESULT-GETTING PROJECTS ←o

1. Examine all of your conscious health habits. Analyze the "cause and effect" action in relation to your physical, mental and spiritual habits in terms of their "healthiness" or "unhealthiness." Determine where, if at all, you are disregarding any sensible, logical concept of good health practice in any of the three areas. Then make a pact with yourself to correct these conditions by changing from negative to positive habits of health. Add the action required of this pact to the program of goals you are working on. This will remove any barrier that may exist today to the presence of consistently good health in your life. Accept this project with an open mind, because there is no other way to relate the ideal of good health to your life. This is also an example of the highest order of control by self-influence.

2. Take a few moments tonight at bedtime to paint a mental picture of yourself as the bright, shiny, healthy person. See yourself being recognized by others as someone cheerful, competent, genial, willing, eager, energetic and the picture of health. Assign this picture to your sub-

conscious mind as the "model" of the kind of a person you want to look like, hereafter. Conduct this kind of a reverie and picture painting for several nights in a row. Then, in a few days begin looking into the eyes of others and you will see that the reflection of you, the person, looks right. And, therefore, it must feel right. You can see the same reflection in your own mirror!

26

You and Your Subconscious Mind as Partners in Action . . . in Relation to Problems

"PROBLEMS! NOTHING BUT PROBLEMS, ONE AFTER ANother!"

You have known people whose viewpoint on life is expressed that way. They are the ones who scowl at the world and accuse it of producing problems for them, "one after another." They are the ones who look at problems as gloomy clouds hanging over their heads. I am sure that you know unhappy people like that, and you tend to sympathize with them.

• Sympathy doesn't solve problems

Perhaps you would be inclined to say, right now: "I do sympathize with them! I know how they feel because I feel that way myself at times." All right, I'll accept the last part of that statement. But I take exception to the "sympathy" idea because

234

it's misplaced in those circumstances. No one with problems needs sympathy. What they do need is. . . . Well, we'll get to that in a moment! First, if you understand that example as being "true life," let's see if this one rings a bell, too.

I am painting a word picture of a little incident that is similar to others in which you have played a part. We see a person sitting in an easy chair, relaxed and apparently contented with himself and the world. We see another person walk up to the relaxed one, and say, "Pretty soft! Boy, I wish I were like you, not a care or problem in the world!" Of course, I should ask you if you have played the part of the *envious observer*, or the part of the *apparently carefree* one. If you have been such an observer and made a statement like that, then I must tell you that your statement is "off the beam!"

• Everybody has problems

If you have been the relaxed one, you should have retorted: "What do you mean 'no problems'? I've got just as many cares and problems as you have!" And it would have been the truth! And if you were really contented with yourself and the world, you would have added: "I've got lots of problems, but I take care of them and they take care of me." If you have not said it, then you should say it in the future, and we'll get to that in a moment, too.

Just what is a problem? Boiled down to essentials, a problem is a question without an easily determined answer! Here's proof. If you are faced with a question, and you find an answer, you have no problem. If you are faced with a question, and there is no apparent answer, you have a problem. Incidentally, these two sentences give you the key to handling problems, any and all problems! Do you see the "key"? Take a guess; you'll probably hit it pretty close. (More "clues" and the "answer" coming up a bit later!)

Do you think that anybody can go through life without coming face-to-face with questions that concern him? Of course not! Well, then, do you think that anyone is ever able to immediately find answers to every question that confronts him? Certainly not! So, it is only simple logic to assume that everybody is going to have problems and have them consistently.

• You can live well with your problems

You can take both comfort and inspiration from that conclusion. It should be comforting to know that everybody else has problems and that you have not been singled out as a particularly bedeviled person. You are right in the swing of things since you have problems like everyone else! But it should also be inspiring to you to relate this fact to the knowledge that life is not the same for everybody, despite the fact that everybody has problems. Even casual observation of people you know indicates that some people live well with their problems while others are overcome by them. These two extremes are pictured in the examples I used at the beginning of the chapter. Inspiration can come from the fact that we know why this difference exists. If you know why some people live well with problems, you can adopt their technique for yourself, and do likewise!

• Concentrate on answers

Going back to those two examples, why the difference? The difference is that the gloomy person with the scowl on his face is concentrating on his problems, while the person who is relaxed and contented is concentrating on the answers to his problems! It's really as simple as that! This works because concentration on the *answers* to problems is the positive approach. When you apply positive action to finding the answers, you are "living well" with your problems. Furthermore, you put this positive technique into operation by starting the action with decision. This produces a "1-2-3" formula for making all problems good problems. You will see that there is nothing complex about this formula.

• Handle all problems "1-2-3"

Step 1. Decide just what the problem is. Simplify it. Eliminate all the fuzzy negative issues that may have become attached to it. Every problem has one basic question, which is the core of it. Identify that core. As soon as you go into action in arriving at this decision, you have put a positive slant on the problem. Failure to do this tends to let the question grow into unwieldy proportions. When this happens, inferiority complexes are often born of the distorted belief that there is no answer to a problem.

Step 2. After you have simplified the problem, decide what the best answer is. There is a best answer to every problem. Often there is a choice of answers, but only one of them will be the best. Talk things over with yourself, even starting out by saying "I could do this, or this, or this." Assign those possible answers to your subconscious for help. But be assured that concentration on the best answer will reveal it to you.

Step 3. Once you have decided on the best answer, act on it! Remember what the "contented" person said: "I've got lots of problems, but I take care of them, and they take care of me." Obviously what he meant was that he acted in response to the positive best answers. As a result, he turned his problems into achievements instead of letting them defeat him.

• Everyone's problems are his own responsibility

About that first example of the person burdened down with problems, you will remember that I said he didn't need sympathy. That could sound as if I didn't feel that this person is in trouble. Certainly he is in trouble, but frankly it is trouble of his own making! Sympathy is not going to help him get out of trouble. It could even tend to make him concentrate more on his problems. What he needs is the cultivation of more faith in himself and the adoption of that "1-2-3" formula. This person himself is the key to whether problems are good or bad in his life, just as it is with you and with everybody else. Again, what is a problem? It's a question without an immediately apparent answer. But between the words "question" and "answer" is the person himself, and his action or lack of it.

• Problems answered equal achievement

Don't make a guessing game out of life by living "poorly" with problems. Make a discovery game of it by seeking the best answer to every problem. Turn problems into achievements by acting on answers.

What does all this add up to? The same universal answer that applies to all factors in a good life. This is the practice of self-influence. The problems are yours, and the answers must be yours. The presence of the first, and the lack of the second, results in a negative influence. But the presence of both results in a positive influence. The conversion depends upon self-influence, so you know that you can find the best answers to problems by turning on this power of subconscious concentration. And now you know that you *can* do it, "1-2-3."

IN SUM

Apply self-influence, i.e., decision and action, to your problems.
Turn them into achievements rather than burdens.
Decide what the problem is.
Decide what the best answer is.
Act on that answer.

o→ RESULT-GETTING PROJECT ←o

Subconscious self-influence cannot be a transitory action in relation to problems. To be effective, it must be as continuous as is the appearance of problems in your life. Therefore, this is not a "one-shot" project. Rather it is something to be adopted as a permanent habit of controlled self-influence. You will begin, of course, by deliberately applying the project to some selected problems of today. But you will anticipate applying it to all problems in the future. This project is as simple as the "1-2-3" formula for conscious action on problems. In fact, it is that formula with the specification, "Assign to your subconscious" applied to each step.

In the process of deciding what a problem really is, assign consideration of it to your subconscious. It will be pleasantly surprising to you to find how effectively this assignment will clear up the question. In the process of deciding the best answer, assign your considerations to your subconscious. Here too, you will discover effective help in establishing priorities that will show the best answer.

When it comes time to act, assign this determination to your subconscious, and let your subconscious be the enthusiastic supporter of your action. Repetition of this pattern of assignment will soon make it the approved way of handling all problems, and you will have acquired a new positive self-influence habit.

27

You and Your Subconscious Mind as Partners in Action ... in Relation to Love

LOVE IS ONE OF THE MOST SIGNIFICANT, FUNDAMENTAL factors in our lives, yet as a community of people recognizing the importance of love, we seem unskillful in demonstrating it.

We put great time and effort in educational programs that develop skills in the arts and crafts, the sciences and the professions. We do this because it is economically intelligent and because it promotes material progress, and that is good. But we do not seem to develop programs that help progress in the art of love. If someone instituted a program entitled "How to Love," I am certain he would have a legion of students, even though conventional society would raise its eyebrows at the thought. Yet such a program would promote moral and spiritual progress.

• You must learn how to love

It would seem that everybody is expected to be on his own in acquiring a knowledge of love that will best serve him during his lifetime. Yes, I know, love is one of the fundamental desires that you want to act upon, and that is the whole point. To have true love in your life, you must follow a pattern of action. The knowledge of the "what, when and how" of that action, is not a fully developed skill you were born with. Perhaps this chapter should be titled "How to Love," because apparently you are expected to perfect the skill of loving and being loved all on your own.

In fact, if in some magic form, I were the "subconscious mind" assigned to work with any one of a number of persons I have known, I would be most confused about this matter of "love" in my master's life. I would be recording his emotional reactions to love quite consistently and, many times, recording his actions as prompted by his emotions. I would build up quite a file of his desire for love, until eventually I took to interpreting it as a great need. I would be ready at any time to remind him of this desire and need and try to back him up whenever he had the chance to act to satisfy the urge to love and be loved.

• A conflict between desire and will

But what would be confusing to me is the *conflicting action* often going on "upstairs" in his conscious mind. Many, many times, there would be a recording up there of an opportunity to satisfy his desire, by demonstrating love, and so I would say, "All right! This is the time! However, there would be *conscious resistance*, strong enough to overcome my influence. As a result, the "action" of my master would be to pass up the opportunity. If this happens many times, I would be forced to build up a "file" of unresponsiveness, and passiveness, because apparently that is the way my master wants to act. But I, as the subconscious, know differently. The emotional desire for active relationships based on love continues to be recorded, but the pattern of consciously influenced action opposes it. It's almost as though my master was consciously saying, "I want to, but I can't!" However, my interpretation of his attitude would be, "I want to, but I won't!" Very confusing!

• Let yourself go, and love!

Furthermore, and still in the face of that desire and need for love that persists in my "files," this conscious passiveness take on the overtones of "no affection" and "no respect." I would know that these are negative reactions, because in this private world of his that is his subconscious, he has great affection and respect for others. You could evaluate his interpretation of love as being a one-way action, with the other person doing all the responding. This, too, would be most confusing to me because, if he just "let himself go" and responded to my best influence, he would be a much happier and more desirable person. I would wish that he and that will of his would quit being so matter-of-fact about love and let me really turn on the power. I would hope that it might happen soon, or I might get "out of the notion." And if "my" power is ever turned off in this matter, this fellow is "dead"!

Of course, I can't substitute for anybody's subconscious and perhaps it's a good thing, for I would be inclined to step out of bounds and really turn the power on, especially in this matter of love! But in this little off-beat "trip into inner space," I have turned the spotlight on a condition that does exist to some degree in the lives of too many persons.

Every man wants the fulfillment in life that comes from active love. This is a basic male desire. And every woman needs love to find true fulfillment in life. Here, too, it is a basic desire. Why, then, does there seem to be such a widespread pattern of conflict between this desire and the expression of love?

• What is love?

I believe that the answer is related to the individual interpretation of what love is and to the knowledge of the consequences of either positive or negative expression of love.

What is love? These, I believe, are the honest definitions: Love is passionate affection between individuals of opposite sex; love is true fondness between individuals of like sex; love is cherishment of one person by another; love is the communion of emotions and affectionate action among people. Without any camouflage, and without any artificial taboos, these are the realistic definitions of love, aren't they? Certainly they are clear enough, and definite enough. However, it is up to each individual to make them have meaning in his or her life, according to the way he or she expresses love.

• Suppressed love is frustrating

If you express love by acting in accordance with those definitions, you are assured of having the positive consequences of love in your life. But if you fail to express love according to those definitions, by restraining or curbing your actions, certainly there will be negative consequences, because, from all practical viewpoints, there will then be no love in your life. Love is a dynamic force when it is the basis for positive, unrestrained action. Love is a frustrating influence when it is kept leashed and passive.

I am sure that you will agree that we have been quite frank, so far. Let us continue in the same spirit, as we explore the consequences of love in the lives of a representative man and woman, either of whom may represent you, wholly or in part.

• Men need a variety of love

Here is a man, intelligent, personable, ambitious and anxious to lead a full life. He may or may not be married. Whatever his status, those four definitions of love are important factors in his life. The man who denies that any part of this is true for him is being dishonest with himself. This man desires and needs that communion between himself and others that is based upon emotion and affection. To have that communion, he must act according to his desires. Unless he so acts, he will still have the desire, but it will remain unsatisfied and frustrating. This man desires to have a feeling of fondness exist between himself and other men, simply because he is a gregarious being, always seeking recognition and acceptance. Such fondness is dependent upon expressive action, and that feeling will exist only when he demonstrates it through action. Failure to demonstrate such fondness can let the bugaboo of rejection appear as the feeling of loneliness.

• A man needs a woman, and love

This man also needs and desires to relate himself to a woman, on the basis of passionate affection. The "object of his affection" will be, of course, his wife or his wife-to-be. Perhaps that phrase "passionate affection" needs to be clarified. "Passionate," in this case, means strong, sure, positive, while "affection" means tenderness and regard. Combine the two, and we have "strong and tender love" as the standard for the relationship between this man and his woman. Is that a right relationship? It most certainly is, if the man acts according to that standard of love, and continues to so act, and *act* AND ACT!

If you are a man, and you are acting according to all of these relationships of love in your life, then you are one whose life is being fulfilled every day! If you are remiss in any of these actions, you cannot deny you have the desire to so act. Get busy on a program of self-influence and let the subconscious desires come out where others can see and feel them. This is the manly thing to do, and you are a man! Incidentally, age doesn't have any bearing on any of this. If you are an adult male, anywhere from 18 to 108, get busy with honest, active love in your life!

• The needs and desires of a woman

And now, a woman, intelligent, attractive, capable, seeking to lead a life of womanly fulfillment. We can picture her, too, as married or unmarried, but with those four definitions of love being vital factors in her life. I am sure that no woman will deny this. With her, as with that representative man, we can go right down the list of those several areas of love, and find that she has the need and desire for them in her life. And, like the man, realization of those desires depends upon positive, expressive action on her part. She will "have or have not," depending entirely upon the demonstrations of her desires, or upon her passiveness.

• Action brings fulfilled love

If you are a woman, and you are acting according to these standards of active love in all of the desired relationships (including the relationships with "the man" in your life), then I know that you are a radiant, happy, contented person! If you don't have fulfillment in all of those relationships where love is a factor, now is the time to call self-influence to the rescue, and let those desires escape from confinement! Believe me, this is the womanly thing to do. Is there any reason why you should not be the "ideal" woman, practicing fulfilled love? And about age (or did you think I wouldn't dare mention "age" and "woman" at the same time?): What does it matter what age you are, as long as there is love in your life? When you are 100— you will still have the same needs and desires for love as you had when you were 18. You won't be silly" if you positively express love as you grow in years. Just think of all the experience you can add to the picture to make active love better as the years go by.

• Love, and be loved, through action

Now let's recall the observations I made at the beginning of this chapter. In that imaginary role as somebody's subconscious mind, I encouraged you to pay heed to those observations about "confusion" and "conflict." I encouraged you to take stock of your own conscious actions in relation to love. Consider what you do, how you act, what you say, in your relationships with those who are closest to you, or intimately related to your life. Do these actions consistently express and demonstrate the love you feel? Consider those desires, deep-rooted within you, to love and to be loved. Are they being suppressed by conscious restraint on your part? Are you consciously creating an attitude of passiveness toward love? If you come up with the "wrong" answers to any of these questions, then you are causing that "confusion" in your subconscious; this is an undesirable, even dangerous, condition which should be corrected. The correction can be made by giving your subconscious the chance to build up more power toward the expression of love. And certainly you know how to accomplish this positive, self-influenced objective.

• There is only one kind of true love

True love is love that is expressed and demonstrated. No one
is more capable of expressing and demonstrating love than you
are. Therefore no one has a greater potential for love in his life
than you have.

True love is an emotional reaction, put into action. Your subconscious is capable of putting great power behind your emotional reactions. Therefore, positive action in relation to love
is assured by self-influenced conditioning of your subconscious.
Therein lies the great opportunity for a fulfilled life for you.

Make true love your kind of love!

IN SUM

Free yourself of all restraints and express your love.

Do this positively, satisfying your subconscious desires.

Love is a dynamic force when it is the basis for
positive, unrestrained action.

Do not allow it to be passive, thus a frustrating influence.

o→ RESULT-GETTING PROJECTS ←o

The ideal influence of true love is habitual influence.
Aim at establishing it as a habit in your life. This is a

seven-day project, based upon planned demonstrations
and expressions of your emotional affection for others. A
variety of people will be the "targets" of your project.
They will be:

1. Your marriage partner, or your intended partner.
2. Men friends, if you are a man, women friends, if you
   are a woman.
3. Persons who are related to you, such as mother or
   father, sister or brother, aunt or uncle.
4. Young children, such as son or daughter, niece or
   nephew, god-child, or other youngsters you know
   well.

These are people who are within that "inner circle" in
your life, where the alliance is based upon the expression
of love according to one or more of the definitions given
in this chapter. These are the people who belong to you,
and to whom you belong.

Giving yourself time to consider this project in a "retreat" atmosphere, designate a day soon when you will
begin this one-week experience. During the preparatory
period, consider all the things you can DO to express and
demonstrate your love to those in each of the four categories. Let yourself mentally "see" an individual, in anticipation of what you are going to do. Consider the things
you haven't done but which you have wanted to do. Assign this intention to act to your subconscious and let
those emotional desires help paint pictures of your action.
Extravagant ideas are not out of order here, since this is
love you are considering. As you do this, you are establishing an objective of demonstrating your love to at least one
person in each category on each day of your week-long
project. Obviously your marriage partner, or your intended, is going to be the object of repeated action, and
that is as it should be. In the other groups, a different person each day is recommended.

At bedtime, on the night before the first day of "action," assign the anticipation of that day to your subconscious and thus let subconscious self-influence prompt you to act the next day. You will act, and you will find that the active expression of love fits into your daily life "as though it belonged there."

Repeat the preparation and subsequent action on the following six nights and six days. As the week progresses, you will find that apparently you need to do less and less deliberate preparation. You will feel that you are "getting into the swing of things" and that the expression of true love is remarkably easy to accomplish. You will be "getting the habit" and, by the end of the week, you will have the habit.

The rewards will be great from this experience, not only because you have removed the restraints from the emotional subconscious desires for love, but also because of the glowing response from others. The men, women and children on your list will prove to you that the expression of love is a two-way action, and, as you give, you will receive.

28

You and Your Subconscious Mind as Partners in Action ... in Relation to Security

APPARENTLY THE MAJORITY OF PEOPLE WISH THAT THEY could have been born with a "guarantee tag" attached to them. The guarantee would read something like this:

"The Creator of this person guarantees that during his life-time he shall have security, above all else. He shall have security against fear, want, danger and uncertainty. This guarantee assures the individual that he will live a smooth, uniform life."

• Security can be guaranteed

I say that apparently most people wish for such a guarantee because of the attitude toward security that has been expressed by so many of our students during the initial analysis period of our classes and home study courses. I have always agreed with their assertions that the ideal life for THEM included security as a major factor. And this should be so for you. I am going to set up a "guarantee" for security in relation to your life, but there isn't going to be anything wishful about it. There will be certain "conditions" related to this "guarantee," but none of them will be related to passiveness.

It was the concept of *passiveness* that many of our students originally had that had kept security from being a major factor in their lives. It was based upon an interpretation of security that defined it simply as a protective shield. I have often felt that many persons would like to live in some kind of a "fortress," impregnable on all sides against "everything." But that idea and the idea that passiveness is the key to security are not logical. They are most illogical when you consider that a human being is born with the capacity to act progressively, aggressively and with freedom. Passive security, or life behind some kind of a protective shield, would isolate a person from even normal life and restrict his actions so that even self-expression and recognition would be eliminated. For these reasons, the Creator wouldn't give anybody the kind of a guarantee that some people wish for. But He does provide the means for everybody to write his or her own guarantee for security, and that includes you!

• Security within and around you

Let us consider the modern-day interpretation of security, in which the influence of today's mode of living is most significant. If you could step back in time and talk to one of our ancient forbears, he would say: "A person is secure if he has a safe place to sleep tonight, a piece of meat for tomorrow's meal and a weapon to protect him from his enemies!" For many of your ancestors, the struggle for security was directly related to self-preservation. It is still related to self-preservation. But in this day and age, security is what makes survival worthwhile. Even in comparatively recent times, two or three generations ago, security was related almost entirely to the control of physical, mechanical and material things. The objective was to provide stronger defensive and protective security. Then, progress among people brought about an awareness of another phase of security that lifted it even above the "certainty of life" interpretation. This new interpretation established security as a dynamic, progressive element which makes life an optimistic adventure. It conceives of security being a force within an individual, as well as around him. It relates security not only to a person's state of being, but also to what he does under the guidance of self-influence.

Because of the progressive, positive elements in our society, the stage has been well set for security around you. You can identify the results of this action as among the blessings of this age in which you live. It has established that element of protective security that you need, provided you identify yourself with the action involved.

• Take advantage of positive environment

Among these elements are: easily available life insurance programs; retirement programs; a forceful national economy that is aimed at the best welfare of everyone; fire, police and health programs; research programs aimed at longer, happier life; and *democracy itself*, with its concept of the high status of each individual. Cooperative sections like these provide for security against fear, want, danger and uncertainty in your environment. They put protective security around you, if you are a part of the action in each case. Desiring, as you do, to live a positive life, I know that you WILL take advantage of all the blessings that this type of security offers, by participation, by support and through faith.

Security around you is good. It is protective and comforting. But more important is the fact that the security provided co-operatively by society relieves you of much of the stress and strain of life that would have been your lot had you lived in an earlier generation. This environmental security relieves the need for concentrating on mere survival and permits you to concentrate on living a full life, with inner security.

• Fight negative forces from within

Inner security is the power to combat negative influences that affect the way you feel, the way you think, the way you react. Inner security is aggressive security as compared to protective security. Inner security is entirely self-induced. It should be apparent to you, therefore, that this calls for action and not retirement in a "darkened cave," hidden from something negative but most unhappy about your weakness. Inner security gives you strength to step forward and combat negative outside influences. Inner security gives you such an advantage over negative influences that you will always come out the victor. Accept this second type of security as part of your plan of life, and you will have at your command both a "defense" and an "offense."

You have inner security and the ability to aggressively beat negative influences to the punch when you are able to do these things: demonstrate your basic faith, know "what to do and when," work on goals that positively budget your life, make life a series of planned achievements, keep the warm fire of happiness burning by your actions, put the influences of heredity and environment in proper perspective, display yourself as a healthy, wholesome person, concentrate on the answers to problems and demonstrate true love. Inner security is the ability to go into self-influenced action in this manner.

• Inner security comes from inner strength

Yes, if you have acquired a clear understanding of the last eleven chapters, in the section related to "You and Your Subconscious Mind as Partners in Action . . . ," then you are building inner security, the inner strength and stability that WILL guarantee the serenity in life that you so greatly desire. As you go forward in your self-influenced life, and when you have acted in accordance with the preceding chapters, you will never have the inclination to "hide" from any negative condition you may have to face.

There isn't much more to be said about security, except this: raise your eyes to the heavens, or bow your head, and in your own way, give thanks for the security that is around you, and for the security that is within you. The person who, from his or her heart, can give thanks, knows what security is!

IN SUM

Inner security can only come from you.

It stems from the knowledge that you have the power to combat negative influences.

Your weapon is a course of positive, self-influenced action.

○➤   RESULT-GETTING PROJECT   ◄○

This project has a very simple and direct objective. It is to be sure that you can and do give thanks for security in your life, in the manner suggested at the end of the chapter. If you have prepared yourself, and you recognize the security that is around you, and if you can feel the fullness of security within you, then do give thanks in a moment of reverence and in such a manner as to impress your subconscious. The warmth of this subconsciously recorded message will come back time and again to cheer you. This is a positive subconscious influence that should be given great status.

If you feel that you cannot yet give thanks, stay with your program of self-influenced control of your life, particularly under the guidance of those last eleven chapters, until you feel that you want to give thanks for the security you feel. And then do so!

29

You and Your Subconscious Mind as Partners in Action ... in Relation to Creativeness and Self-expression

"IN THE BEGINNING GOD CREATED THE HEAVEN AND THE earth. . . ."

For much of mankind, those words, recorded in Genesis almost 6,000 years ago, have been ever since, the basis for interpretations of relationships with the Creative Spirit. They have undoubtedly been related to your own interpretation through your religious faith.

I am going to put an interpretation on them that is directly related to your concept of self-influence. This interpretation is related to a partial summary of most theological and philosophical interpretations which is, in brief: "Since God created this world and all things in it, including humans, He is our

Father and we are His children. As His children, we have both obligations and opportunities. But above all, all things begin and live because of the Creative Spirit. Therefore all things begin and end with God. This has always been and will always be."

• You are a creative being

Now I am going to add to that interpretation and put a slant on it that I hope will "hit home," insofar as you are concerned. Since you were created by this Master Creator and since you are part of His creative scheme of things, *you* are endowed with a natural aptitude for creativeness! Creativeness is both the source and the power of life. You have life and, therefore, you have the power of creativeness.

• What's new with you?

Are you using this power and this aptitude? Are you using it to help satisfy those urges for recognition and achievement, to satisfy that great need you have for self-expression? How often has something like the following happened to you? You meet someone who greets you with: "What's new?" You come back with: "Brother, let me tell you what's new!", and you proceed to tell about the new sales idea you put across, or a new idea of yours that your club is working on or any new idea of yours that is being used. Do you ever give such an enthusiastic response to "What's new?" If you don't, I know that it isn't because you don't have good ideas. You have good ideas in abundance but unless they are being used, they haven't much value.

Just "having" good ideas isn't being creative in the dynamic sense that pays off. To create means to originate and produce. You must produce your ideas, get them into use, otherwise who knows or even cares if you have them? Who has the responsibility for producing them? (Tip: the answer is to be found on the first page of the second chapter.) People who don't produce good ideas are the ones who say: "I wish I had thought of that" or: "I have a pretty good idea, but somebody else has probably beat me to it." These are the kind who throw away their aptitude for creativeness and "starve" themselves for lack of recognition and achievement.

Good ideas—produced and put to use—result in action that is the highest form of self-expression. All it takes is self-influenced action to capitalize on the aptitude you have for creativeness. Creativeness and self-influenced action on good ideas are effective tools for self-expression, "straight across the board," in your life.

• Try out your good ideas

First, there is that obvious field of invention and improvement in the world of mechanical and material things. You may never be concerned vocationally with this field, but I am reminded of the many useful and profitable contributions that have been made by laymen in the technical progress of our country. So, don't sit on any idea you may have in this field. At least try to produce it. I am pretty sure that the best "mouse trap" has not been made as yet!

• Be creative about relationships

Then there is the need for creativeness in relationships with people. A good creative job as a program chairman, where you *produce* and put your ideas into use, will be appreciated by your club or group, and be a highlight experience in self-expression. Creating harmony, creating good-will, creating enthusiasm, among your associates, simply means producing your good ideas. You could almost have a full time job in this field, you and your creativeness.

• Meet competition with creativeness

Another field where creativeness in action is almost a necessity is in meeting competition. You can't avoid competition, and I'm sure you wouldn't want to. If you had no competition in your endeavors, you would probably be such a "lone wolf" that people by the dozens would avoid you! But good ideas, produced and put to use, will always keep you at least level with your competition and will help you surpass it often enough to make life more interesting!

• Good ideas often save the day

Creativeness is also effective when circumstances or conditions around you get into "bogged down" state. These are the times when others do not seem to know "where to turn next," or they frantically hope that something or somebody will come along with an idea for putting things right again. Ideas seem to be scarce at such times, or so others say! The person who saves the day, and become the "hero," can very well be you, if you will just take an objective look at the situation. You are creative! You will come up with a good idea, and you will produce it, and it will be used, provided you use the power of self-influence first. You can do that!

Yes, you have the "point" now! Creativeness is follow-through on good ideas. But producing an idea sometimes takes a bit of practice. Sometimes you have to kick an idea around a bit so that it is "born" healthy and strong. In fact, this is highly recommended so that you make no false starts when you do produce an idea. I am sure I don't have to remind you that the place to prepare good ideas for production is in your subconscious mind.

Some people are credited with having an over-abundance of originality and imagination. But I think that most of them are simply using the power of their subconscious to amplify their good ideas. Certainly, this is what you can and should do. When you see a right time and place for the application of one of your good ideas, assign the basic idea to your subconscious and let it get polished up so that it comes out ready for first-class production.

• Produce your good ideas

There is one more field where creativeness and self-expression are teamed up. This has to do with a subject entitled, *Your Subconscious Power—How to Make It Work for You.* Yes, this whole book of yours is based upon "good ideas," and you have a creative relationship to every one of them. The whole process of your experience in this, your book, is based upon creativeness, which means, of course, the producing of those ideas and the action of putting them to use by that creative being, you! Furthermore, the net result of this true creativeness is a continuous demonstration of self-expression, again with you as the subject.

From these facts you can draw a conclusion that forecasts a life-time experience for you, in productive creativeness and in stimulating self-expression. This forecast is based upon your present objective, which is to shape a progressive, self-influenced life for yourself. This objective is supported by creativeness and self-expression. Therefore, a life-time relationship of these factors is assured.

Yes, through self-influenced action, you are creating a new model of yourself. And you are building a new plan of living for yourself, one in which you will express yourself according to the highest standards.

In view of what has come to you through your latest experiences, would you not say that God created a pretty good world? I am sure you would, and I add, He created a pretty fine person, in you!

IN SUM

You have a natural aptitude for creativeness.
You have an innate desire to express yourself.
Putting your ideas into action uses that aptitude to satisfy that desire.
Use your power of the subconscious to amplify your ideas.

● ● ●

SUMMARY OF PART THREE
PERFECTION

- You have built an inner security.
- It guarantees your desired serenity in life.
- You have a clear understanding of you and your subconscious as partners in action.
- Basically, your security stems from your newly acquired ability to express your innate power of creativeness.
- This is to say that you now have the security and the ability to counteract the negative influences about you and in you.
- You will do this through action.

● ● ●

PART FOUR

A NEW LIFE

30

A New Model of You, a More Important Person

ALL THE PRACTICE PROJECTS HAVE NOW BEEN COVERED, and all those special projects attended to. Here you are, like a "senior" on commencement day.

This is truly a great day for you, and I wish I could share it with you in person. I would like to meet you, fresh from your recent experiences. I would shake your hand and say, "Well, let me take a look at you now!" But I don't have to be with you to know what I would see. I know I would see a more important person than the one I met in Chapter 1, although *both* would be you!

• Congratulations to a more important person

Your change in status was inevitable. It was forecast at the moment you signed your name in this book, back there at the beginning. And now you are more important—more important to the world and more important to yourself. All this has happened because of what you have done, through self-influenced action. You had guidance, of course, but you were the one who made a dynamic interpretation of that guidance. You were the one who brought yourself to this point of perfection, and I congratulate you.

Back in Chapter 7, we had quite a discussion of the "latest models in human beings." Of course, I don't know what particular model, or combination of them, you agreed was the description of yourself at that time. But I am certain that you chose one special model as the one that would describe you sometime in the future. I am sure I don't need to remind you of the description of that ideal model since it, and probably some additional features you have added, has been your subconsciously held objective ever since. But right now, I have an *objective* in mind as I review that description with you. I would be surprised if you had no emotional reactions as you read along with me.

• How do you compare with that ideal model?

We described this ideal model as a person who is going along steadily and surely on a program of his own making. We said that he is able to make choices that comprise his program, that they fit together admirably with the activities of the world about him. We said that his program of living is basically self-influenced, but that he never fails to use the best outside influences to his advantage. We said that, when desirable, he was able to influence other people and his environment. We said that life is no mystery to him and that he actively supports the progressive programs that are aimed at making this a better world. We also said that certainly he is a candidate for that "master race" of progressive, important people.

What were your emotional reactions as you read that description of a person? I am pretty sure I know what they were. You felt as though you were standing in a spotlight, reading a "citation" about yourself, and you felt that it was true!

• That new, better model is you

And that brings me to my objective. You will recall that once before I said: "You are today what you have done in the past." I repeat that now and tell you that it applies perfectly here. What you have done in the recent past, through your dedication to the projects in this book and through your dedication to self-influenced action, has made you what you are today. That description fits you today; it is you we have just read about!

You have reached this point of perfection because you have made your subconscious mind your partner in action. The world about you is now adjudging you as a "more important person" purely on the basis of what you have recently *done* and what you are now *doing*. Other people who are important to you are measuring and evaluating your actions and your attitudes, as expressed in action. Their reaction to your actions is causing them to say, "Here is a fine person, worth knowing and cultivating." This evaluation by others, and the resultant judgments, will continue as long as you live. If you are to maintain your "more important" status, then certainly your actions must continue on the same level as now. And so, we come right back to that same basic premise that started this whole experience for you, and that is the standard of importance you set up for yourself. The obvious answer is for you to maintain and strengthen that partnership with your subconscious. This self-influence factors that brought you to this perfected point, must be used again and again to keep you there. There is no doubt that you will use them, is there?

• The many attributes of this new model

Here are the "self" factors that have made you "more important."

You have self-assurance, and you have used it to motivate your positive actions. Continue!

You have self-confidence, and you have used it to overcome negative influences through positive action. Continue!

You have self-determination, and you have used it to take you toward your goals, through positive action. Continue!

You have self-reliance, and you have used it to guide you in making positive decisions. Continue!

You have self-sufficiency, and you have used it to cause stimulating interpretations of what a good LIFE really means. Continue!

You have self-respect, and you have used it to put the right value on your "net worth" as a person. Continue!

You have practiced self-expression, and found it to be a rewarding experience, approved by others. Continue!

And you have self-control, and you have used it positively and aggressively. Continue!

• Keep using subconscious self-influence

Yes, you are more important now because of self-influenced action. The difference between this recent action and action that may have come from self-influence in the past is that it is all positive action. It is the result of concentrated positive self-influence. It happened because of that partnership you established with your subconscious. So when I suggest that you continue to use and depend upon those self factors, I know that I am suggesting something that you understand and have already put on the priority list in your life. Subconscious self-influence brought you to this desirable status, and it will keep you there, always!

• Thank you!

Certainly you should have an "award" on this, your "graduation," day. I suppose it could be some kind of a certificate or plaque. But in my opinion, neither would indicate the true value of your accomplishment. However, I can give you something else in recognition of this personal achievement, something that is highly treasured by other people who have it and greatly envied by those who do not have it. This is the appreciation and thanks of the world for the contributions you make to it, as a better person. We, who live in the world with you, applaud you for your self-made standards of accomplishment. We know that this will be a better world only as there are better people living here. You have made yourself a better person, and everyone of us will benefit from your active part in life, as this better person. We thank you!

• Great expectations ahead

But, also speaking for "the world," let me tell you that now we expect great things of you! Of course that is what you expect of yourself. So while we have our eyes on you, you will have a watchful eye on yourself. I have no doubt that this *new model* of you will get better and better, in the stimulating future that is just ahead!

IN SUM

You and your subconscious—your partner in action —have made you a new person.

Continue to use your subconscious.

You and the world will be better for it.

A project for this chapter? Yes, turn the page, and put that future into action!

31

A Plan for Living
for this New You

THE FUTURE, YOUR FUTURE! BRIGHT AND CLEAR, ISN'T IT? "You are today what you have done in the past." What you are doing today is positive, progressive and right for you. So when today becomes "yesterday," and the future becomes the present, it, too, will be a day of rightness for you! That is the pattern of the future for you. What is more, the promise of this bright future is warmly affecting the present, for when the future is bright, the present is bright, also! All of this puts you on a happy "merry-go-round" of life! So now your objective is to stay on it and keep it going!

● You have planned a bright future!

Is there a plan of living that will assure this positive daily action and a bright, optimistic future? Yes, there is, for someone like you. That plan is right at hand. Thumb through your book.

270

There is the basis for the plan. Finger those papers, notes, bookmarks, written plans that you have made in relation to your practice projects. All of these represent examples of the plan in action. Your book and those examples of self-influenced action perfectly fit the new model of you. In fact, these brought about the new model. Therefore your plan of life will simply be "more of the same."

• You will always do these positive things

Since action is the key to the successful application of this plan, let me remind you of the keys to control of that action. Using these as the foundation of your plan will assure the use of all of the auxiliary factors that support positive action. These keys, you remember, are:

1. The creed of "do, positively," the creed that calls for action, performance, production and accomplishment.

2. The three rules of (a) deliberately conditioning your subconscious by what you do consciously; (b) wholeheartedly wanting the best outcomes from self-influenced action; (c) letting your subconscious have free reign in demonstrating its great power.

3. Establishment of a pattern of personal "retreats" in your life, where you can concentrate on your purpose in life and looking at your progress objectively.

4. Seeking guidance, and the use of all of the readily available resources to equip you with practical, usable knowledge of positive living.

5. Keeping your program full of positive, progressive action by having several goals in prospect, on a variety of subjects, at the same time.

6. Taking advantage of the full capacity of your subconscious to serve you, by deliberately giving this inner mind of yours positive projects to work on, even while you sleep.

• That promised perfection

These are the bases for that positive plan of living that you have already demonstrated as being the ideal for you. Perfection, through the perpetuation of this plan, is at hand for you in being a self-influenced person of importance. Perfection is at hand in that important intimate sphere of life that is your home, your family, your friends, your work associates. Perfection is at hand for you in that necessary sphere of life that has to do with material wants and needs, with financial success and the increase of your net worth. Perfection is at hand in the use of the power of your subconscious. Perfection is at hand in all of the facets of life that are important to your happiness, success and contentment. This state of perfection will be preserved through continued self-influenced action. This perfection is assured because you know how to always keep self-influence on the positive side.

At this moment, I would like to put you up on top of a high tower, so you could survey the big, dynamic world you live in. I would say to you, "Look all about you! This is your world, and you are now one of its most important people! Act accordingly!"

I know you will act accordingly. And you know you will!

IN SUM

You have planned a new life.
You have planned a bright future.
Perfection is at hand.

A final project? There certainly is! The project is . . . **your** future . . . positively self-influenced!

● ● ●

SUMMARY OF PART FOUR
A NEW LIFE

- You, with your new power of self-influence, are a changed person.
- Your future will be just what you want it to be.
- Remember, this is your world.
- You are now one of its most important occupants.
- *Act accordingly.*

● ● ●

PART FIVE

PRACTICE PROJECTS

PRACTICE PROJECT ONE

MASTER SELF-INFLUENCE PLAN

Circled here are the three personal goals I want most, and that I will achieve, in my new, positive, self-influenced life:

I	Accomplishment Dates			II	Accomplishment Dates		
	Month	*Day*	*Year*		*Month*	*Day*	*Year*
Time	____	__	__	Love	____	__	__
Money	____	__	__	Content-			
Energy	____	__	__	ment	____	__	__
Health	____	__	__	Peace of			
The Future	____	__	__	Mind	____	__	__
				Adventure	____	__	__
				Beauty, or			
				Looking			
				My Best	____	__	__

III	Accomplishment Dates		
	Month	*Day*	*Year*
Achievement	____	__	__
Recognition	____	__	__
Self-Expression	____	__	__
Personality	____	__	__
Happiness	____	__	__

This list is a source of power to you. It shows you what you can and will do now . . . tomorrow . . . next week . . . next year. Be sure to keep this paper with you . . . read it just after rising and before going to bed.

PRACTICE PROJECT TWO

THE NEW POSITIVE CONCEPT OF LIFE MASTERY (*"Self-Control"*)

Here are the two keys that will help me use the power of my subconscious mind, to achieve the three goals circled on Practice Projects One:

1. I will deliberately control my conscious actions, keeping them always positive. This is the way I will build up my *subconscious* file of positive actions.

2. I will change negative habits by deliberately and consciously cultivating positive habits to take their place. (I remember that I can't erase anything in my subconscious.)

Keep these "keys" handy! You will use them more and more!

PRACTICE PROJECT THREE

THE THREE RULES FOR NEW SUBCONSCIOUS POWER

The more I use this formula every day, the sooner I will achieve the three personal goals for my new, positive life, which I circled on Practice Projects One:

1. (Major goal) For achieving my major goal I will deliberately condition my subconscious by what I do consciously.

2. (For achieving my deadline goal) I will wholeheartedly want the best results from such self-influenced action.

3. (For achieving my step-by-step goals) I will let my subconscious have free reign in demonstrating its power. I will let new, exciting things happen to me, knowing that they will happen to me.

PRACTICE PROJECT FOUR

A BUDGET OF LIFE

Fit This "Goal-Control" Into Your Other Practice Projects

1. Major goals first. Establish positive, progressive goals you already have (in Chapter 6).

2. Alternative goals are important. You may switch to these anywhere along the line without losing ground, if circumstances require a change.

3. Use timetables for progress. As soon as each goal is established, put a timetable alongside of it. *Be definite* about how, where, and when. Remember, your subconscious *wants* specifics to work on.

4. Never turn back. Anticipate meeting obstacles, but anticipate *overcoming* them.

5. Variety is necessary. Budget your life with a variety of goals. "The more the merrier" is the way your subconscious looks at goals.

6. Sell your goals to others. Let everyone know who should know that you have established your aims in life, that this is going to be your new life.

Use these six goal makers and your skill in budgeting your life will increase day by day! (Now turn to the next Practice Project)

PRACTICE PROJECT FIVE

Write your goals here (don't forget that your subconscious will help you to achieve as many goals as you give it):

1. Major goal _____   *I will accom-*
   plish this goal
   by   _____ __ __
           month   day   year

    Alternative goal _____   *I will accom-*
   plish this goal
   by   _____ __ __
           month   day   year

2. Major goal _____   *I will accom-*
   plish this goal
   by   _____ __ __
           month   day   year

    Alternative goal _____   *I will accom-*
   plish this goal
   by   _____ __ __
           month   day   year

3. Major goal _____   *I will accom-*
   plish this goal
   by   _____ __ __
           month   day   year

To score a bull's-eye on these goals, keep your "sights" on them and keep firing!

PRACTICE PROJECT SIX

MY SUCCESS PATTERN

	Action	Planned	Achieved
Success *Achievements*		☐	☐
		☐	☐
		☐	☐
My Goals		☐	☐
		☐	☐
		☐	☐

List the *actions* involved in your practice steps (or in any other action where you called the shots).

List everything you can think of that you "planned" and "achieved" and put a check mark after each item in both columns. As fast as you make an achievement in relation to any goal, or any step toward that goal, mark it in the "achieved" column.

Ahead of you are more achievements, and more success as you continue to make things happen.

This is the life pattern of a successful person—*you!*

PRACTICE PROJECT SEVEN

HOW TO CREATE HAPPINESS THROUGH SELF-INFLUENCE

1. Give of yourself.
2. Look for the bright side.
3. Act purposefully.
4. Establish and maintain a working relationship with your God.
5. Seek peace of mind.

Look for opportunities to do these kinds of things on a chosen day. You'll find you can have the same happy experiences *every* day!

PRACTICE PROJECT EIGHT

SELF-INFLUENCE VERSUS HEREDITY AND ENVIRONMENT

	Good	Need Improvement	Heredity	Environment
Personal Appearance				
Use of good judgment				
Decision making				
Getting along with others				
Optimistic viewpoint				
Follow-through on plans				
Cheerfulness				
Influence over others				
Influence over self				
Self-expression				

This inventory should prove to you how much power you really have to change your life!

PRACTICE PROJECT NINE

Here's How You Handle Problems 1-2-3

. . . memorize these simple steps:

Step 1. Decide just what the problem is. Simplify it. Eliminate all fuzzy negative issues. Identify the core question. This proves that there *is* an answer to your problem.

Step 2. After you have simplified the problem, decide what the best answer is. There is a best answer to every problem.

Step 3. Once you have decided on the best answer . . . *act* on it! Act in response to the positive best answers . . . and turn problems into *achievements*.

PRACTICE PROJECT TEN

REMEMBER THESE SIX GUIDES FOR A PLANNED, PURPOSEFUL LIFE:

1. Do, positively, the creed that calls for action, performance, production and accomplishment.
2. Deliberately condition your subconscious by what you do consciously. Wholeheartedly want the best outcomes from your actions. Let your subconscious have free rein in demonstrating its great power.
3. Establish in your life a pattern of personal "retreats" where you concentrate on your purpose in life, and look at your progress objectively.
4. Seek guidance, and use all of the readily available resources to equip you with practical, usable knowledge of positive living.
5. Keep your program full of positive, progressive action by having several goals in prospect, on a variety of subjects, at the same time.
6. Take advantage of the full capacity of your subconscious to serve you by deliberately giving your inner mind positive projects to work on, even while you sleep.

This is the basis for the positive plan of your life!

MELVIN POWERS SELF-IMPROVEMENT LIBRARY

ASTROLOGY

___ ASTROLOGY: HOW TO CHART YOUR HOROSCOPE *Max Heindel*	5.00
___ ASTROLOGY AND SEXUAL ANALYSIS *Morris C. Goodman*	5.00
___ ASTROLOGY AND YOU *Carroll Righter*	5.00
___ ASTROLOGY MADE EASY *Astarte*	5.00
___ ASTROLOGY, ROMANCE, YOU AND THE STARS *Anthony Norvell*	5.00
___ MY WORLD OF ASTROLOGY *Sydney Omarr*	7.00
___ THOUGHT DIAL *Sydney Omarr*	7.00
___ WHAT THE STARS REVEAL ABOUT THE MEN IN YOUR LIFE *Thelma White*	3.00

BRIDGE

___ BRIDGE BIDDING MADE EASY *Edwin B. Kantar*	10.00
___ BRIDGE CONVENTIONS *Edwin B. Kantar*	10.00
___ COMPETITIVE BIDDING IN MODERN BRIDGE *Edgar Kaplan*	7.00
___ DEFENSIVE BRIDGE PLAY COMPLETE *Edwin B. Kantar*	15.00
___ GAMESMAN BRIDGE—PLAY BETTER WITH KANTAR *Edwin B. Kantar*	7.00
___ HOW TO IMPROVE YOUR BRIDGE *Alfred Sheinwold*	7.00
___ IMPROVING YOUR BIDDING SKILLS *Edwin B. Kantar*	7.00
___ INTRODUCTION TO DECLARER'S PLAY *Edwin B. Kantar*	7.00
___ INTRODUCTION TO DEFENDER'S PLAY *Edwin B. Kantar*	7.00
___ KANTAR FOR THE DEFENSE *Edwin B. Kantar*	7.00
___ KANTAR FOR THE DEFENSE VOLUME 2 *Edwin B. Kantar*	7.00
___ TEST YOUR BRIDGE PLAY *Edwin B. Kantar*	7.00
___ VOLUME 2—TEST YOUR BRIDGE PLAY *Edwin B. Kantar*	7.00
___ WINNING DECLARER PLAY *Dorothy Hayden Truscott*	7.00

BUSINESS, STUDY & REFERENCE

___ BRAINSTORMING *Charles Clark*	7.00
___ CONVERSATION MADE EASY *Elliot Russell*	5.00
___ EXAM SECRET *Dennis B. Jackson*	5.00
___ FIX-IT BOOK *Arthur Symons*	2.00
___ HOW TO DEVELOP A BETTER SPEAKING VOICE *M. Hellier*	4.00
___ HOW TO SAVE 50% ON GAS & CAR EXPENSES *Ken Stansbie*	5.00
___ HOW TO SELF-PUBLISH YOUR BOOK & MAKE IT A BEST SELLER *Melvin Powers*	20.00
___ INCREASE YOUR LEARNING POWER *Geoffrey A. Dudley*	3.00
___ PRACTICAL GUIDE TO BETTER CONCENTRATION *Melvin Powers*	5.00
___ 7 DAYS TO FASTER READING *William S. Schaill*	7.00
___ SONGWRITERS' RHYMING DICTIONARY *Jane Shaw Whitfield*	10.00
___ SPELLING MADE EASY *Lester D. Basch & Dr. Milton Finkelstein*	3.00
___ STUDENT'S GUIDE TO BETTER GRADES *J. A. Rickard*	3.00
___ TEST YOURSELF—FIND YOUR HIDDEN TALENT *Jack Shafer*	3.00
___ YOUR WILL & WHAT TO DO ABOUT IT *Attorney Samuel G. Kling*	5.00

CALLIGRAPHY

___ ADVANCED CALLIGRAPHY *Katherine Jeffares*	7.00
___ CALLIGRAPHY—THE ART OF BEAUTIFUL WRITING *Katherine Jeffares*	7.00
___ CALLIGRAPHY FOR FUN & PROFIT *Anne Leptich & Jacque Evans*	7.00
___ CALLIGRAPHY MADE EASY *Tina Serafini*	7.00

CHESS & CHECKERS

___ BEGINNER'S GUIDE TO WINNING CHESS *Fred Reinfeld*	5.00
___ CHESS IN TEN EASY LESSONS *Larry Evans*	5.00
___ CHESS MADE EASY *Milton L. Hanauer*	5.00
___ CHESS PROBLEMS FOR BEGINNERS *Edited by Fred Reinfeld*	5.00
___ CHESS TACTICS FOR BEGINNERS *Edited by Fred Reinfeld*	5.00

___ HOW TO WIN AT CHECKERS *Fred Reinfeld*	5.00
___ 1001 BRILLIANT WAYS TO CHECKMATE *Fred Reinfeld*	7.00
___ 1001 WINNING CHESS SACRIFICES & COMBINATIONS *Fred Reinfeld*	7.00

COOKERY & HERBS

___ CULPEPER'S HERBAL REMEDIES *Dr. Nicholas Culpeper*	5.00
___ FAST GOURMET COOKBOOK *Poppy Cannon*	2.50
___ HEALING POWER OF HERBS *May Bethel*	5.00
___ HEALING POWER OF NATURAL FOODS *May Bethel*	5.00
___ HERBS FOR HEALTH—HOW TO GROW & USE THEM *Louise Evans Doole*	5.00
___ HOME GARDEN COOKBOOK—DELICIOUS NATURAL FOOD RECIPES *Ken Kraft*	3.00
___ MEATLESS MEAL GUIDE *Tomi Ryan & James H. Ryan, M.D.*	4.00
___ VEGETABLE GARDENING FOR BEGINNERS *Hugh Wiberg*	2.00
___ VEGETABLES FOR TODAY'S GARDENS *R. Milton Carleton*	2.00
___ VEGETARIAN COOKERY *Janet Walker*	7.00
___ VEGETARIAN COOKING MADE EASY & DELECTABLE *Veronica Vezza*	3.00
___ VEGETARIAN DELIGHTS—A HAPPY COOKBOOK FOR HEALTH *K. R. Mehta*	2.00
___ VEGETARIAN GOURMET COOKBOOK *Joyce McKinnel*	3.00

GAMBLING & POKER

___ HOW TO WIN AT DICE GAMES *Skip Frey*	3.00
___ HOW TO WIN AT POKER *Terence Reese & Anthony T. Watkins*	7.00
___ SCARNE ON DICE *John Scarne*	15.00
___ WINNING AT CRAPS *Dr. Lloyd T. Commins*	5.00
___ WINNING AT GIN *Chester Wander & Cy Rice*	3.00
___ WINNING AT POKER—AN EXPERT'S GUIDE *John Archer*	5.00
___ WINNING AT 21—AN EXPERT'S GUIDE *John Archer*	7.00
___ WINNING POKER SYSTEMS *Norman Zadeh*	3.00

HEALTH

___ BEE POLLEN *Lynda Lyngheim & Jack Scagnetti*	3.00
___ COPING WITH ALZHEIMER'S *Rose Oliver, Ph.D. & Francis Bock, Ph.D.*	10.00
___ DR. LINDNER'S POINT SYSTEM FOOD PROGRAM *Peter G. Lindner, M.D.*	2.00
___ HELP YOURSELF TO BETTER SIGHT *Margaret Darst Corbett*	7.00
___ HOW YOU CAN STOP SMOKING PERMANENTLY *Ernest Caldwell*	5.00
___ MIND OVER PLATTER *Peter G. Lindner, M.D.*	5.00
___ NATURE'S WAY TO NUTRITION & VIBRANT HEALTH *Robert J. Scrutton*	3.00
___ NEW CARBOHYDRATE DIET COUNTER *Patti Lopez-Pereira*	2.00
___ REFLEXOLOGY *Dr. Maybelle Segal*	5.00
___ REFLEXOLOGY FOR GOOD HEALTH *Anna Kaye & Don C. Matchan*	7.00
___ 30 DAYS TO BEAUTIFUL LEGS *Dr. Marc Selner*	3.00
___ YOU CAN LEARN TO RELAX *Dr. Samuel Gutwirth*	3.00

HOBBIES

___ BEACHCOMBING FOR BEGINNERS *Norman Hickin*	2.00
___ BLACKSTONE'S MODERN CARD TRICKS *Harry Blackstone*	5.00
___ BLACKSTONE'S SECRETS OF MAGIC *Harry Blackstone*	5.00
___ COIN COLLECTING FOR BEGINNERS *Burton Hobson & Fred Reinfeld*	7.00
___ ENTERTAINING WITH ESP *Tony 'Doc' Shiels*	2.00
___ 400 FASCINATING MAGIC TRICKS YOU CAN DO *Howard Thurston*	7.00
___ HOW I TURN JUNK INTO FUN AND PROFIT *Sari*	3.00
___ HOW TO WRITE A HIT SONG & SELL IT *Tommy Boyce*	7.00
___ MAGIC FOR ALL AGES *Walter Gibson*	4.00
___ STAMP COLLECTING FOR BEGINNERS *Burton Hobson*	3.00

HORSE PLAYER'S WINNING GUIDES

___ BETTING HORSES TO WIN *Les Conklin*	7.00
___ ELIMINATE THE LOSERS *Bob McKnight*	5.00
___ HOW TO PICK WINNING HORSES *Bob McKnight*	5.00

___ HOW TO WIN AT THE RACES *Sam (The Genius) Lewin*	5.00
___ HOW YOU CAN BEAT THE RACES *Jack Kavanagh*	5.00
___ MAKING MONEY AT THE RACES *David Barr*	5.00
___ PAYDAY AT THE RACES *Les Conklin*	5.00
___ SMART HANDICAPPING MADE EASY *William Bauman*	5.00
___ SUCCESS AT THE HARNESS RACES *Barry Meadow*	5.00

HUMOR

___ HOW TO FLATTEN YOUR TUSH *Coach Marge Reardon*	2.00
___ HOW TO MAKE LOVE TO YOURSELF *Ron Stevens & Joy Grdnic*	3.00
___ JOKE TELLER'S HANDBOOK *Bob Orben*	7.00
___ JOKES FOR ALL OCCASIONS *Al Schock*	5.00
___ 2,000 NEW LAUGHS FOR SPEAKERS *Bob Orben*	7.00
___ 2,400 JOKES TO BRIGHTEN YOUR SPEECHES *Robert Orben*	7.00
___ 2,500 JOKES TO START 'EM LAUGHING *Bob Orben*	7.00

HYPNOTISM

___ ADVANCED TECHNIQUES OF HYPNOSIS *Melvin Powers*	3.00
___ CHILDBIRTH WITH HYPNOSIS *William S. Kroger, M.D.*	5.00
___ HOW TO SOLVE YOUR SEX PROBLEMS WITH SELF-HYPNOSIS *Frank S. Caprio, M.D.*	5.00
___ HOW TO STOP SMOKING THRU SELF-HYPNOSIS *Leslie M. LeCron*	3.00
___ HOW YOU CAN BOWL BETTER USING SELF-HYPNOSIS *Jack Heise*	4.00
___ HOW YOU CAN PLAY BETTER GOLF USING SELF-HYPNOSIS *Jack Heise*	3.00
___ HYPNOSIS AND SELF-HYPNOSIS *Bernard Hollander, M.D.*	5.00
___ HYPNOTISM *(Originally published in 1893) Carl Sextus*	5.00
___ HYPNOTISM MADE EASY *Dr. Ralph Winn*	5.00
___ HYPNOTISM MADE PRACTICAL *Louis Orton*	5.00
___ HYPNOTISM REVEALED *Melvin Powers*	3.00
___ HYPNOTISM TODAY *Leslie LeCron and Jean Bordeaux, Ph.D.*	5.00
___ MODERN HYPNOSIS *Lesley Kuhn & Salvatore Russo, Ph.D.*	5.00
___ NEW CONCEPTS OF HYPNOSIS *Bernard C. Gindes, M.D.*	10.00
___ NEW SELF-HYPNOSIS *Paul Adams*	7.00
___ POST-HYPNOTIC INSTRUCTIONS—SUGGESTIONS FOR THERAPY *Arnold Furst*	5.00
___ PRACTICAL GUIDE TO SELF-HYPNOSIS *Melvin Powers*	5.00
___ PRACTICAL HYPNOTISM *Philip Magonet, M.D.*	3.00
___ SECRETS OF HYPNOTISM *S. J. Van Pelt, M.D.*	5.00
___ SELF-HYPNOSIS—A CONDITIONED-RESPONSE TECHNIQUE *Laurence Sparks*	7.00
___ SELF-HYPNOSIS—ITS THEORY, TECHNIQUE & APPLICATION *Melvin Powers*	3.00
___ THERAPY THROUGH HYPNOSIS *Edited by Raphael H. Rhodes*	5.00

JUDAICA

___ SERVICE OF THE HEART *Evelyn Garfiel, Ph.D.*	10.00
___ STORY OF ISRAEL IN COINS *Jean & Maurice Gould*	2.00
___ STORY OF ISRAEL IN STAMPS *Maxim & Gabriel Shamir*	1.00
___ TONGUE OF THE PROPHETS *Robert St. John*	7.00

JUST FOR WOMEN

___ COSMOPOLITAN'S GUIDE TO MARVELOUS MEN Foreword by *Helen Gurley Brown*	3.00
___ COSMOPOLITAN'S HANG-UP HANDBOOK Foreword by *Helen Gurley Brown*	4.00
___ COSMOPOLITAN'S LOVE BOOK—A GUIDE TO ECSTASY IN BED	7.00
___ COSMOPOLITAN'S NEW ETIQUETTE GUIDE Foreword by *Helen Gurley Brown*	4.00
___ I AM A COMPLEAT WOMAN *Doris Hagopian & Karen O'Connor Sweeney*	3.00
___ JUST FOR WOMEN—A GUIDE TO THE FEMALE BODY *Richard E. Sand, M.D.*	5.00
___ NEW APPROACHES TO SEX IN MARRIAGE *John E. Eichenlaub, M.D.*	3.00
___ SEXUALLY ADEQUATE FEMALE *Frank S. Caprio, M.D.*	3.00
___ SEXUALLY FULFILLED WOMAN *Dr. Rachel Copelan*	5.00

MARRIAGE, SEX & PARENTHOOD

___ ABILITY TO LOVE *Dr. Allan Fromme*	7.00
___ GUIDE TO SUCCESSFUL MARRIAGE *Drs. Albert Ellis & Robert Harper*	7.00
___ HOW TO RAISE AN EMOTIONALLY HEALTHY, HAPPY CHILD *Albert Ellis, Ph.D.*	7.00
___ PARENT SURVIVAL TRAINING *Marvin Silverman, Ed.D. & David Lustig, Ph.D.*	10.00
___ SEX WITHOUT GUILT *Albert Ellis, Ph.D.*	5.00
___ SEXUALLY ADEQUATE MALE *Frank S. Caprio, M.D.*	3.00
___ SEXUALLY FULFILLED MAN *Dr. Rachel Copelan*	5.00
___ STAYING IN LOVE *Dr. Norton F. Kristy*	7.00

MELVIN POWERS' MAIL ORDER LIBRARY

___ HOW TO GET RICH IN MAIL ORDER *Melvin Powers*	20.00
___ HOW TO SELF-PUBLISH YOUR BOOK & MAKE IT A BEST SELLER *Melvin Powers*	20.00
___ HOW TO WRITE A GOOD ADVERTISEMENT *Victor O. Schwab*	20.00
___ MAIL ORDER MADE EASY *J. Frank Brumbaugh*	20.00

METAPHYSICS & OCCULT

___ CONCENTRATION—A GUIDE TO MENTAL MASTERY *Mouni Sadhu*	7.00
___ EXTRA-TERRESTRIAL INTELLIGENCE—THE FIRST ENCOUNTER	6.00
___ FORTUNE TELLING WITH CARDS *P. Foli*	5.00
___ HOW TO INTERPRET DREAMS, OMENS & FORTUNE TELLING SIGNS *Gettings*	5.00
___ HOW TO UNDERSTAND YOUR DREAMS *Geoffrey A. Dudley*	5.00
___ IN DAYS OF GREAT PEACE *Mouni Sadhu*	3.00
___ MAGICIAN—HIS TRAINING AND WORK *W. E. Butler*	5.00
___ MEDITATION *Mouni Sadhu*	10.00
___ MODERN NUMEROLOGY *Morris C. Goodman*	5.00
___ NUMEROLOGY—ITS FACTS AND SECRETS *Ariel Yvon Taylor*	5.00
___ NUMEROLOGY MADE EASY *W. Mykian*	5.00
___ PALMISTRY MADE EASY *Fred Gettings*	5.00
___ PALMISTRY MADE PRACTICAL *Elizabeth Daniels Squire*	7.00
___ PALMISTRY SECRETS REVEALED *Henry Frith*	4.00
___ PROPHECY IN OUR TIME *Martin Ebon*	2.50
___ SUPERSTITION—ARE YOU SUPERSTITIOUS? *Eric Maple*	2.00
___ TAROT *Mouni Sadhu*	10.00
___ TAROT OF THE BOHEMIANS *Papus*	7.00
___ WAYS TO SELF-REALIZATION *Mouni Sadhu*	7.00
___ WITCHCRAFT, MAGIC & OCCULTISM—A FASCINATING HISTORY *W. B. Crow*	7.00
___ WITCHCRAFT—THE SIXTH SENSE *Justine Glass*	7.00

RECOVERY

___ KNIGHT IN RUSTY ARMOR *Robert Fisher*	5.00
___ KNIGHT IN RUSTY ARMOR *Robert Fisher (Hard cover edition)*	10.00

SELF-HELP & INSPIRATIONAL

___ CHARISMA—HOW TO GET "THAT SPECIAL MAGIC" *Marcia Grad*	7.00
___ DAILY POWER FOR JOYFUL LIVING *Dr. Donald Curtis*	7.00
___ DYNAMIC THINKING *Melvin Powers*	5.00
___ GREATEST POWER IN THE UNIVERSE *U. S. Andersen*	7.00
___ GROW RICH WHILE YOU SLEEP *Ben Sweetland*	7.00
___ GROW RICH WITH YOUR MILLION DOLLAR MIND *Brian Adams*	7.00
___ GROWTH THROUGH REASON *Albert Ellis, Ph.D.*	7.00
___ GUIDE TO PERSONAL HAPPINESS *Albert Ellis, Ph.D. & Irving Becker, Ed.D.*	7.00
___ HANDWRITING ANALYSIS MADE EASY *John Marley*	7.00
___ HANDWRITING TELLS *Nadya Olyanova*	7.00
___ HOW TO ATTRACT GOOD LUCK *A.H.Z. Carr*	7.00
___ HOW TO DEVELOP A WINNING PERSONALITY *Martin Panzer*	7.00
___ HOW TO DEVELOP AN EXCEPTIONAL MEMORY *Young & Gibson*	7.00
___ HOW TO LIVE WITH A NEUROTIC *Albert Ellis, Ph.D.*	7.00
___ HOW TO OVERCOME YOUR FEARS *M. P. Leahy, M.D.*	3.00
___ HOW TO SUCCEED *Brian Adams*	7.00

____ HUMAN PROBLEMS & HOW TO SOLVE THEM *Dr. Donald Curtis*		5.00
____ I CAN *Ben Sweetland*		8.00
____ I WILL *Ben Sweetland*		7.00
____ KNIGHT IN RUSTY ARMOR *Robert Fisher*		5.00
____ KNIGHT IN RUSTY ARMOR *Robert Fisher (Hard cover edition)*		10.00
____ LEFT-HANDED PEOPLE *Michael Barsley*		5.00
____ MAGIC IN YOUR MIND *U.S. Andersen*		10.00
____ MAGIC OF THINKING SUCCESS *Dr. David J. Schwartz*		7.00
____ MAGIC POWER OF YOUR MIND *Walter M. Germain*		7.00
____ MENTAL POWER THROUGH SLEEP SUGGESTION *Melvin Powers*		3.00
____ NEVER UNDERESTIMATE THE SELLING POWER OF A WOMAN *Dottie Walters*		7.00
____ NEW GUIDE TO RATIONAL LIVING *Albert Ellis, Ph.D. & R. Harper, Ph.D.*		7.00
____ PSYCHO-CYBERNETICS *Maxwell Maltz, M.D.*		7.00
____ PSYCHOLOGY OF HANDWRITING *Nadya Olyanova*		7.00
____ SALES CYBERNETICS *Brian Adams*		10.00
____ SCIENCE OF MIND IN DAILY LIVING *Dr. Donald Curtis*		7.00
____ SECRET OF SECRETS *U.S. Andersen*		7.00
____ SECRET POWER OF THE PYRAMIDS *U. S. Andersen*		7.00
____ SELF-THERAPY FOR THE STUTTERER *Malcolm Frazer*		3.00
____ SUCCESS-CYBERNETICS *U. S. Andersen*		7.00
____ 10 DAYS TO A GREAT NEW LIFE *William E. Edwards*		3.00
____ THINK AND GROW RICH *Napoleon Hill*		8.00
____ THREE MAGIC WORDS *U. S. Andersen*		7.00
____ TREASURY OF COMFORT *Edited by Rabbi Sidney Greenberg*		10.00
____ TREASURY OF THE ART OF LIVING *Sidney S. Greenberg*		7.00
____ WHAT YOUR HANDWRITING REVEALS *Albert E. Hughes*		4.00
____ YOUR SUBCONSCIOUS POWER *Charles M. Simmons*		7.00
____ YOUR THOUGHTS CAN CHANGE YOUR LIFE *Dr. Donald Curtis*		7.00

SPORTS

____ BILLIARDS—POCKET • CAROM • THREE CUSHION *Clive Cottingham, Jr.*	5.00
____ COMPLETE GUIDE TO FISHING *Vlad Evanoff*	2.00
____ HOW TO IMPROVE YOUR RACQUETBALL *Lubarsky, Kaufman & Scagnetti*	5.00
____ HOW TO WIN AT POCKET BILLIARDS *Edward D. Knuchell*	7.00
____ JOY OF WALKING *Jack Scagnetti*	3.00
____ LEARNING & TEACHING SOCCER SKILLS *Eric Worthington*	3.00
____ MOTORCYCLING FOR BEGINNERS *I.G. Edmonds*	3.00
____ RACQUETBALL FOR WOMEN *Toni Hudson, Jack Scagnetti & Vince Rondone*	3.00
____ RACQUETBALL MADE EASY *Steve Lubarsky, Rod Delson & Jack Scagnetti*	5.00
____ SECRET OF BOWLING STRIKES *Dawson Taylor*	5.00
____ SOCCER—THE GAME & HOW TO PLAY IT *Gary Rosenthal*	7.00
____ STARTING SOCCER *Edward F. Dolan, Jr.*	3.00

TENNIS LOVER'S LIBRARY

____ HOW TO BEAT BETTER TENNIS PLAYERS *Loring Fiske*	4.00
____ PSYCH YOURSELF TO BETTER TENNIS *Dr. Walter A. Luszki*	2.00
____ TENNIS FOR BEGINNERS *Dr. H. A. Murray*	2.00
____ TENNIS MADE EASY *Joel Brecheen*	5.00
____ WEEKEND TENNIS—HOW TO HAVE FUN & WIN AT THE SAME TIME *Bill Talbert*	3.00

WILSHIRE PET LIBRARY

____ DOG TRAINING MADE EASY & FUN *John W. Kellogg*	5.00
____ HOW TO BRING UP YOUR PET DOG *Kurt Unkelbach*	2.00
____ HOW TO RAISE & TRAIN YOUR PUPPY *Jeff Griffen*	5.00

The books listed above can be obtained from your book dealer or directly from Melvin Powers. When ordering, please remit $2.00 postage for the first book and 50¢ for each additional book.

Melvin Powers
12015 Sherman Road, No. Hollywood, California 91605